The phrase 'know your onions' means that you are an expert in your field, top of your game and you really know your stuff

BIS

BIS Publishers
Building Het Sieraad
Postjesweg 1
1057 DT Amsterdam
The Netherlands
T (31) 020 515 02 30
F (31) 020 515 02 39
bis@bispublishers.nl
www.bispublishers.nl

ISBN 978 90 6369 312 1

Printed in China

3230216975

For Fitzroy

Design: www.navig8.co.uk
Typeset in good old Bembo with a splash of Bodoni
and a dollop of Helvetica condensed

KNOW YOUR ONIONS

WEB DESIGN

CONTENTS

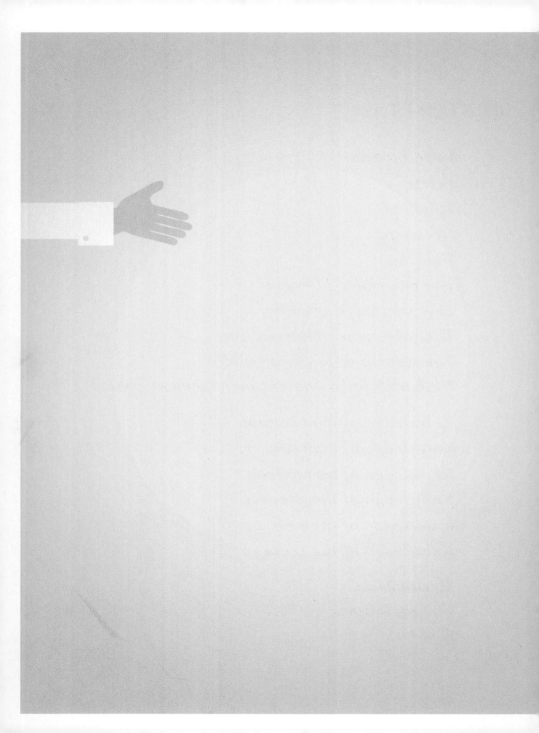

INTRODUCTION

I recognise that it might seem odd to write a book about web design and not just build a website about web design. The feedback I've had about my previous book: *Know Your Onions: Graphic Design* was that people kinda liked having it beside their computer, making notes and spilling Frappuccino all over it, so a book it is.

Let's get something straight from the start. This book is not the be all and end all of web design. I received a rather fabulous duffing up in the form of a review for my last book, *Know Your Onions: Graphic Design* because the content wasn't detailed enough. Each chapter, subject and activity in this book could be a book on its own, and there are books out there, some from this very same publisher, that tackle these subjects in detail. This book does not do that; it would be huge if it did. So for instance, **I'm not going to go into any depth on design for tablets or smart phones or responsive design, agile, scrum** or other athletic sounding activities – they may turn out to be books of their own.

Know Your Onions: Responsive Web Design *has a certain ring to it, don't you think?*

If you wanna know how to design a great website that people might actually use, then this book will do the trick.

The World Wide Web is a fast-moving entity and things change all the time, without resorting to statements like 'this book is accurate at the time of going to press, typical 4% APR, your home is at risk if you do not keep up your payments'. I have tried to focus on what makes good design great and not too many examples of websites and technology that will, inevitably, become out of date. You may come across some things as you go through the book that you might want to learn more about, or simply get an up-to-the-minute 'technology-check'. If in doubt, do a search and look it up online.

My background, setting aside minor altercations with the authorities, is in graphic design. Like most companies, my design agency, Navig8, tackles design for print, branding, web and everything in between. I've kind of grown up with the internet. I remember us getting our first email address at the agency I worked at and having no clue what on earth anybody was talking about, or how it worked. The only time I saw an @ sign was on a greengrocer's bill. So I am going to assume, my dear readers, and dear you are to me, that you have some basic understanding of what's out there on the World Wide Web and that you want to grasp the principles of great interactive design and mash up some serious pixel action. I have included some sections on how it all works, because I realise some of the terminology and technology only makes sense to developers and it will help you to understand what happens 'under the hood'. This book has no coding in it, it's not going to teach you how to build a site, but it will teach you how to understand their structure and design websites so that people actually know how to use and buy stuff, or whatever it is you are trying to get them to do.

I've primarily focused on designing web pages for the real world, because that is what most of us do. Mobile apps, email widgets and the downright bonkers, experimental interfaces have their place in the ever changing world, but I do not consider them the main strength of this book.

Whether you are a print designer, student, graduate or balloonist, you will need to think very differently about web design than you might for other design disciplines. Web designers are like architects, you might have a vision for an amazing building, but a load of other people will be involved and you will have to wait a while to get the thing built. Print designers, on the other hand, tend to work on their own and it only takes a few days to get your hands on your spanking new printed brochure.

As a web designer, you will have to understand a stack of things and be aware of activities that you may not actually end up doing yourself. It will be somebody else's job. As I say, it's a bit like being an architect; you don't need to be a brick-layer, or know how to patina copper to build a beautiful building, but you do have to know how it can be done and by whom.

WHAT YOU MIGHT LEARN:

Things that you will hopefully get from this book:

- How to question each project brief and start thinking for yourself and your client.
- How to define and understand functionality and make sure the specifications are right.
- Unleash your creativity to help you design fast and effectively.
- Get your head around the different types of website structure.
- Understand the issues and importance of navigation systems and how to design them.
- Understand the particular issues when designing for Content Management Systems.
- Learn about colour, fonts and using images.
- Best practice for project management.
- Getting your designs ready for the development team.
- Understand web conventions.
- Learn about content types.
- Understand how servers, domains and all the bits fit together to make a website work.
- Understand the web design and build process.
- Learn about architecture and wireframes.
- Find out who does what in the web development team.

BRIEFS

So, how to begin? Somebody, I think he was Chinese, said: "Every thousand mile march starts with one step". A typical web project is certainly a journey, and often a long one. A good project delivers a result that is a marriage of a client's needs, users' desires and the designer's talent (not to mention the developer's skill). Indeed, every marriage starts with a proposal, and both a marriage and a web project will offer you a long and rocky journey. But let's deal with the first steps and the proposal first.

In order for you to build a strong proposal (getting down on one knee is not usually necessary), you will need to question the brief.

Let's make some assumptions. You have a client, they want a website, they have a company. OK, but that does not make a brief. So before you start, it is likely you will be sent either a brief or a Request For Proposals (RFP) or a tender.

What's the difference between the three? Not a huge amount, but broadly speaking:

A **brief** outlines what the client would like to achieve with the site, who they are, who the users of the site will be and an outline of the spec. A brief under most circumstances, does not include detailed enough information to give you a deep understanding of the site's function. This is a top level document for you to respond to, question and provide a ball-park estimate.

Briefs: a word also used for knickers, panties and pants.

An **RFP** is usually a more formal document, perhaps with a slightly more in-depth specification included. Companies often request proposals from a few different agencies and usually ask for costing, schedules and the like.

A **tender** is a request requiring a highly detailed response. These are often lodged on procurement websites for larger projects and any number of agencies to respond to. This can be a procurement requirement, usually because the final budget for the web project is high and the organisations have guidelines to help ensure a fair and open bidding process.

Most tenders ask for solutions to be put forward and this is often unpaid. You and your agency need to decide if you are happy to put this effort in to win the contract. I don't believe anyone should offer work for free, but with projects of this size, it is unlikely the client will feel confident in your ability if you do not illustrate a response to their brief. Be sure of one thing (actually, two things): tenders require a lot of work, so don't bother starting one unless you know in your heart of hearts that you can win.

It's a sad, sad reality that on occasion you will be asked to tender for something that, no matter how good your proposal is, you are never going to win. Sometimes the organisation just goes through the process because they have to, which is very annoying as they have already chosen the agency they want to use. You can spot when this happens because they will usually tell you that you were not successful because, "we decided to use the incumbent agency because we felt they understood our brand more".

No matter what you are responding to, you will need to question the 'brief'. In the next section, I will give you some projects to get the old grey matter thinking about what the possibilities and considerations might be. Every scenario will, of course, be different.

A website brief template is a jolly good place to start and you can download this for free from the website: knowyouronions.info

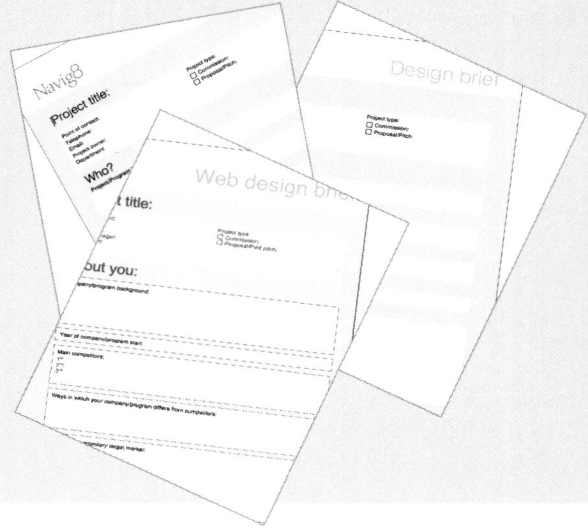

NOTES AND SKETCHES

THINKING

Everything you design has to 'do' something. A business card for example 'does' something, it says something about you and the company you work for. But a business card has a low-level, short-term interaction. It goes like this – "Hello, my name is Drew, I am a Director of a design group called Navig8, here's my card", and Jocasta takes my card, feels the quality of the paper, looks at the design, and makes a judgement. That just about covers the interactivity of a business card.

With a website, there is way more stuff going on. For starters, it is rare that people just arrive at you or your client's site; they will probably have come from a variety of sources. They may have been given your business card, or searched for something they are looking for, or they may just have heard about the site. Either way, they already have a purpose, and that purpose is gold. That is your brief and, depending where they have come from and what they want to do, and what kind of person they are, it underpins everything you want to achieve.

Purpose: the reason these people visit your site, combined with the kind of user they are, gives you a clear vision of what the site should be and do.

Try to think this way from now on; you have to be in the mindset of your client's customers, *they are the brief.* Give them what they want and you are on to a winner.

I'll give you four diverse examples of imaginary web design projects that will help you understand how to define your brief with your client and think about what you could do. In my experience, with web design, the more questions you have asked and understood the answers at the beginning, the more likely you will design an amazing and effective website.

Project one: **Accountancy firm**
Project two: **Band**
Project three: **Charity**
Project four: **Gentleman's outfitter**

I've picked these four because they cover a lot of bases and a good range of likely scenarios – something that could be a brochure site, something cool, something that needs to address a number of issues and something that has products or services.

Each project and website has specific needs to make it successful. They all have competitors, they all want their website to 'do' something for them, but they are all different. You can make them better – and that is the rub.

Project one: Accountancy firm

OK, project one. This is probably the hardest one as accountants have websites because they think they should, not because they think a website is part of the business model or will do anything useful. Most will have pictures of people in business environments with very white teeth, in meeting rooms working on solving difficult accounting type problems. Their sites list their services, might even have a picture of their partners. Erm, what else?

This is what we call a brochure site. It's an OK gig, sure – you will make it look nice, but to be honest, brochure sites are there for show and not much else. When Winston (top accountant) meets a new potential client, he'll hand over his business card – said client will maybe look at his website when they get back to the office and see the company does 'tax advice' or 'forensic accounting' and either decide to contact them or not. Be careful, forensic accounting is not as exciting as it sounds. Don't go thinking your client will be attending murder scenes and performing on-the-spot tax advice that may solve a murder.

If Winston and his company are really good, they will send out a newsletter, informing people about important tax issues, like a change in government policy or some interesting tax issue that means you can only claim your suit on expenses if you are an astronaut or some other interesting government 'initiative' that helps businesses not make money.

But most of the time, the site does nothing. It sits there, being mildly cheaper than a brochure, slowly getting out of date until a senior partner in a law firm becomes embarrassed enough because the site is out of date, heinously ugly, and commissions a new site.

Two things you can do here – accept it, design it and leave it. Or, try to highlight the potential of the new site and offer them something that will help their business and their clients. A website, for almost any business, can perform a business-enhancing task. It can make money or make the day-to-day business activity easier. As I sit here, I can't think of one business that wouldn't benefit from an internet activity to expand their offering. See if you can think of one. By questioning your client, you will either incite them to look at their business in a different light, or annoy them. If you question the brief and get a positive response from the client, you may have a client for life.

It is worth repeating that; something that will help *their* business (your client) and your client's clients, will help build a long-term relationship with you, because you have added value and done something over and above what you have been asked to do.

In this instance, I'm going to assume that your client has told you all they want is five web pages that say: who we are, what we do, contact us, who we work for and the terms and conditions. But what if...

What if...

Let's look at it from the accountant's *client* point of view, not from the accountant's point of view... what if, like me, I have company accounts for ten years, what if... I could have them stored in a secure, password protected place on my accountant's website, so that when I get asked to provide company particulars by suppliers, the last three years of accounts and all that other stuff, I had a place where it would all be kept, online, in date order, just for me.

What if... as a designer, your whole life should be a questioning, creative journey of 'what ifs'.

What if... I had an accountant who knows I own a second property (I wish) and eight employees. The site could serve content that might interest me, or at least put something in the monthly email that might make my finger hesitate over the delete button when it arrives in my inbox.

It's a 'what if'... But if the internet has done one thing, it has made even the most unlikely businesses make an effort. A company can communicate directly with a customer and effectively give them what they need.

This is what I want from my accountant's website, and I don't get it from mine:

- All my accounts online in a secure area, downloadable in PDF and Excel format.
- Management accounts when they are ready.
- VAT and Tax projections – giving me a calendar so I know when to pay.
- A calendar detailing payments due, with email alerts.
- An executive summary giving me my turnover, profit before tax and after tax for every year.
- My VAT liability for each quarter.
- Oh my life, what if I could get a quarterly review and predict my cash flow!

Of course some of this comes with accounting packages, but they stand alone on Sheila's computer, our bookkeeper, and that's not the same.

My accountant has these things to hand, it should be no great shakes for him. I doubt any accountant does this for their client. These things can all be delivered in an automated way and all add value to the accountancy business.

This is all good for designers, even if it is something of an uphill struggle. Try talking to them and, as I say, have a go and if you don't get anywhere, sit down and try making a silk purse out of a sow's ear. As you may have guessed, the reason for this case study is to try to get you guys to not accept the inevitable and at least have a go and think what you could do with a site, which on the face of it, is a site that does nothing.

I gave you a few pointers earlier, here's a few more, and they are all 'what ifs'.

What if... the interface served different content depending on the client type? We talk a bit more about this later, we call it 'user journeys'. For instance, some accountants specialise in certain types of clients. If their favourite clients are rap stars (we all need tax advice) then the rap artist could click on a button just for them, and the content would suit their needs. "Yo, yo, word, dis tax on yo rims is whack, if Ay list em as the rides' repairs, the man can't get his hands on your cheese" – or whatever, I may not have got the vernacular right.

What if... your company had its own page, that you accessed through a password that not only listed your accounts, but had a calendar to warn you about when your income tax is due, your expenses needed to be in, etc. – you'd probably like that. It would effectively remember all the things most of us business owners don't really want to bother with remembering – we'd really find that useful.

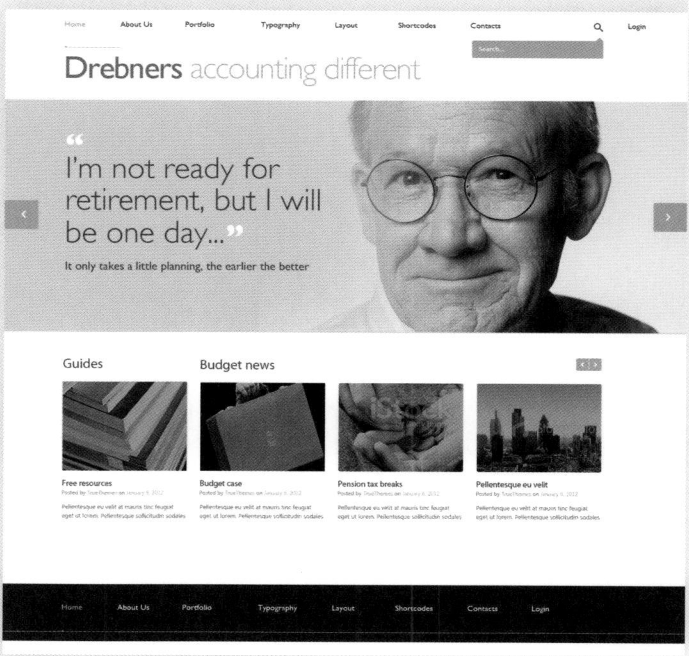

I hope you get the idea. Apply this thought process to *every* project. On to the next one.

TRY THIS:

- Spend half an hour thinking about all the cool things the websites you like do.
- Now, think how you could integrate these cool things into an accountant's website. Tough one. But get it right, or at least get some of it right, and your accountant's website will be a million times better than the one down the road.
- How did you get on?

Project two: Band

This type of project, working with a cool band, is most web designers' dream job. Most bands will have sorted themselves out with an online presence with free services like a MySpace site, a Facebook profile or even a WordPress site. So delivering an 'official site' isn't as easy as it sounds because a lot of the work has already been done. These free sites offer an amazing amount of functionality. There are ways of integrating all these sites and elements into 'the official site', and I will go though them, as much as I can, but for now, I'm trying to get you through the early design process.

Assuming you have listened to the music, and nobody cares if you like it, by the way – just say you do – then you should have some sense of what style the site should incorporate. This is the beginnings of the brand. It's no good designing a black site with flaming text and religious iconography if your band plays medieval ballads. Actually, that might work. But there is a tendency for designers to design sites that they like and they have seen elsewhere, as opposed to something that the fan base wants.

Two things to think about when designing a band site – if they are famous already, it's all about maximising sales, selling tour tickets and tackling the international market. Even if 'your' band isn't a global phenomenon and is struggling away to get noticed, then selling tickets to a live show still applies. Getting Facebook 'likes', building a bigger fan base by letting the fans feel closer to the band, whilst tempting record companies and the powers that be to notice them, is important. There are two distinct markets here; the punters and the suits. Your design should accommodate both.

Hang on Drew, you are talking about functionality here. That's someone else's job, isn't it? It is, but not all of the time. In fact, not most of the time. A good designer has to deal with not only how things look, but also how they work. It's not such a bad thing after all.

Actually, this is an important point. If you are a print designer, a lot of the time you are given the content and you design around it. But being a web designer, you are closer to being a product designer than a print designer in many ways. You have to consider how it works, what it does and what the user's experience is.

Websites for bands tend to be graphic rich, have lots of great images and less live text. As you can see from the example below, it's a fair few years old, but I still like it and I still like the band!

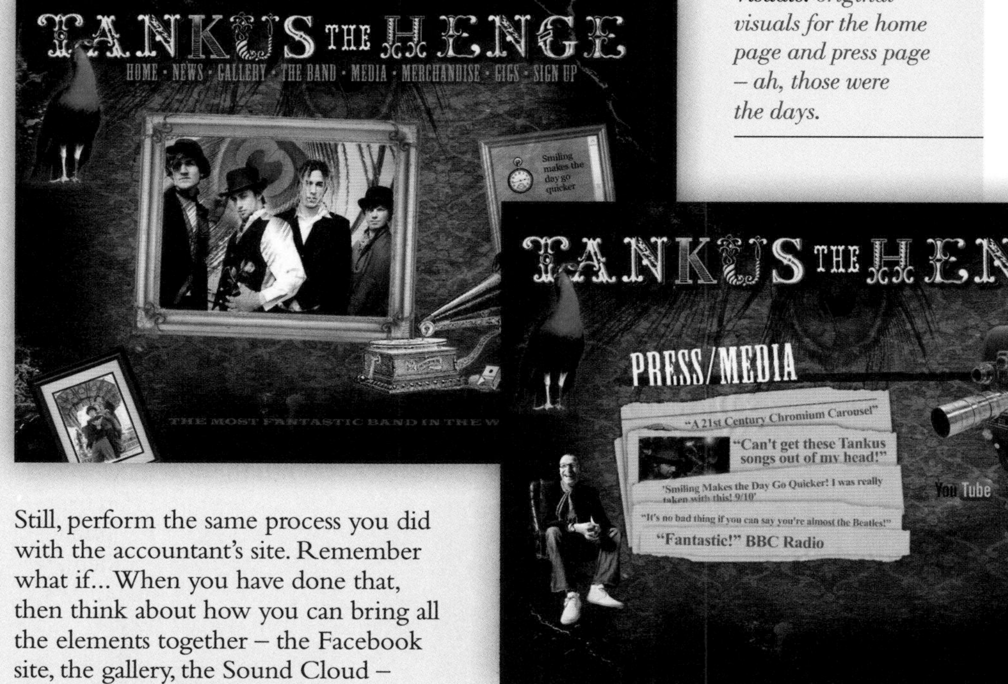

Visuals: original visuals for the home page and press page – ah, those were the days.

Still, perform the same process you did with the accountant's site. Remember what if... When you have done that, then think about how you can bring all the elements together – the Facebook site, the gallery, the Sound Cloud – everything, so that the official site becomes the one place anybody and everybody, who has any interest in the band visits, and finds what they want to find. Bands old and new rarely understand the importance of this. Get it right and the band sell more tickets, sell more songs and...

In effect a charity that does its job, works to remove the problem it has defined, then it is working itself out of a job. If they succeed in their aims and help the 'people' who need support and get the government (or whatever causes the problem) to put in place the policies to eradicate or ease the issue, then the charity is no longer needed – just a thought...

Project three: Charity

All of the previous practices apply and that is the point of this bit of the book. Go through the process again, what if... How do I bring it all together? How do I get the style right so that the site is on brand? Done that yet? If not, go back to the beginning and cover those points, then move on.

Charities have very different agendas from accountants and bands. First of all, there isn't usually a lot of money to play with and – most charities, and I say most – because every charity client is different – have three things they need a site to do. These tend to be: get donations to help them continue their work, actually deliver the work and campaign for change.

There is one other activity that a charity often wants, and that is to provide support to the 'people' who need it. (People are in inverted commas here because if the charity looks after stray dogs, it is unlikely, if not newsworthy, that the dog will login to the website to find the best kennel near them.)

So, if your new charity website gets the brand right, provides the functionality all of their users' needs and wants and brings all the elements together – there is a thing that nearly all charity sites need a user to do, it's called a 'call to action'.

It's a term that applies to lots of different things, in the charity world it is usually a campaign action like emailing a politician, signing up to a cause, making a donation to that cause, or all of the above.

So, this project needs the content and the design to help the charity get their users to follow that user journey, understand the issue and perform the call to action. Like this.

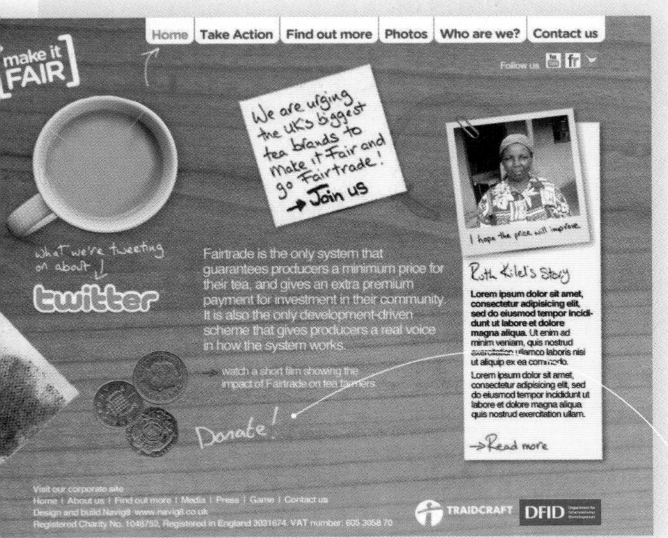

Issue

The government ignores the fact that even in this modern day and age, children in wealthy countries still live in poverty. These children have little hope or opportunity of breaking the cycle. They will remain poor, grow up and may do naughty things, things they feel they have to do because they are poor. Things like 'borrowing' things from shops, and spitting, or even worse.

Charity site purpose/message

"Listen up people, this shouldn't be happening. Sign up to our petition to get the government to take this issue seriously. Give us a bit of 'dolla' so we can spend it on campaigning to get the government to listen, and we will also spend a bit helping the people in this predicament."

I've broken it down here into easy chunks but, essentially, it is what it is. If you are designing a website to do what the charity needs to do, you need to think about the message and the action. Way before you start choosing colours and gawd knows what.

So, design the site, the pages and the communication, to deal with this issue. I'll tell you how later, but for now, think about it.

Progress: not all progress is good. The top example is a design from years ago, with a clear message and call to action. Below the up-to-date site. I don't know where to look!

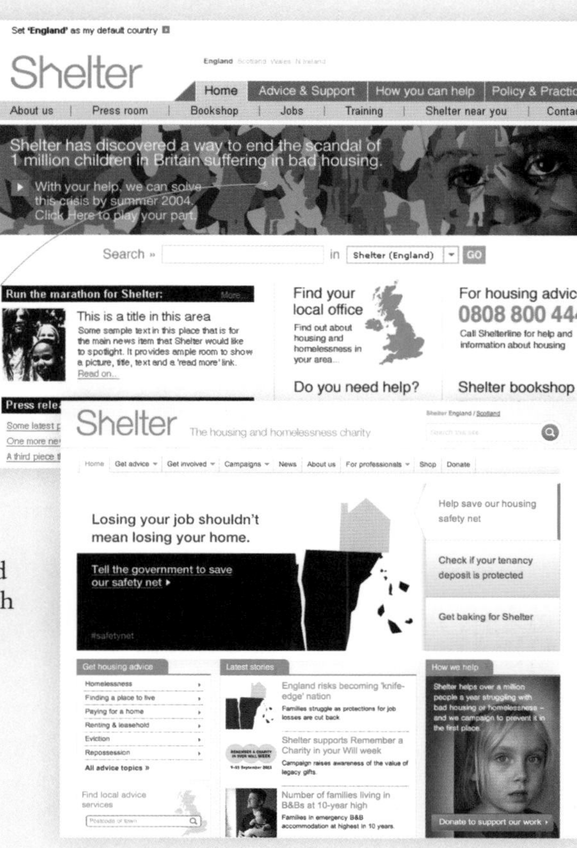

Clear campaign messages and a clear call to action, but the search position is perhaps not quite right.

Project four: Gentleman's outfitter

Again, all of the above. What if... How can I bring it all together? What about the brand? What is the call to action?

A large proportion of the websites that most graphic designers end up working on, are those that basically provide information. The examples I've listed previously give information about the company, information you might be interested in, information about policy, information about gigs. Information is great, but there is no interaction.

When designing websites, things change when people are trying to sell something. Again, all of the above applies when thinking about the project, what if... etc. But things are more complex when transactions are involved and the stakes are way higher. I'll explain why briefly, as you'll get annoyed and you probably just want to get on with the design bit and don't care what the digital marketeers think.

It is worth considering, even if it's just for a mo. If you are selling fine silk cravats, hand linked socks (I don't know what linked is, but I think it is good) and pocket squares, you have to compete with all the other gentleman's outfitters websites out there. The internet creates competition and an even playing field.

So if your client's site is to succeed, it needs to work much harder than the competition, whilst appearing to be much simpler and easier to use.

For this project, I will illustrate the usual points above, but in reverse order, in the box below.

HAVE A GO AT:

- What's the call to action?
- Is it on brand?
- How can I bring it all together?
- What if?
- How did you get on?

The user's journey is very important when you want to sell somebody something and keep on selling to them in future. Users need to instinctively know what to do next and actually 'feel' they 'need' to buy that cravat.

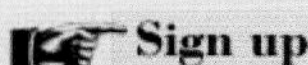

Call to action: a respectable example of a call to action, but not the most inspiring... how could it be better? These below could be all part of the same brand.

Let's first look at identifying the problems, again, in the reverse order.

What's the call to action?
The problem: "How do I get my customers and potential customers to engage (and keep engaging) with my site?"

How can I get them to recommend my site or share and talk about it?

What will make them come back for more? Notice, I didn't say buy more.

The easy thing is of course to get them to buy, but that is only one way to engage with a website. If this is all you came up with, you are not taking this seriously enough and you should burn this book and consider working as a toll collector in one of those booths.

There are a few more calls to action and other ways to engage people that you might like to consider: you can ask them to sign up for news and offers, recommend a friend, build a wish list, 'like' on Facebook, etc.

Is it on brand?
This can be a big problem, but this book isn't called 'Know Your Onions: Branding', which would be an excellent book, but for now I will keep it simple. Let's assume your Gentleman's outfitter has some kind of corporate identity. Perhaps a logo, colour scheme and a strap-line like 'Furnishing the

sartorial gentlemen with clothes befitting the modern age", a tad long for a strap-line, but hey.

How does the site – the user experience, the graphics and the text – reflect the brand? Before we go any further, just a quick note on brand. Brand is not the same as corporate identity. It's not just the logo. Some agencies profess to provide a service called 'branding' and what they actually do is design the client a logo and call it branding. A logo is part of a corporate identity and a corporate identity is a small part of a brand. A brand consists of many parts, some of which are very difficult to pin down. George Clooney is a brand, as are you, my dear reader. Brand encompasses how an organisation might speak about its products, their tone of voice, or even what their customers might say about their products. Take this re-working of our gentleman's outfitters strap line for a typical software giant: "Furnishing users with software befitting the modern age" – err, no. Our gentleman's strap line suits the brand of a quirky gentleman's outfitter. It does not suit a software giant. A good and true strap line for a software giant might be, "Releasing software full of bugs and forcing our customers to upgrade".

Window shopping Sir?

Register today to save your preferred items for another day. Rather like a 'wish list' if you will...

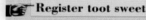

Register toot sweet

Content as well as design needs to strike the right tone. It can really add personality to a website.

A good brand gets every single bit right, so that every action, word and product supports and builds that brand. A company's brand encompasses the style of its packaging, and even how its customers talk about it! Big stuff.

It's fairly clear the type of design approach that a company like our example might want. What is the right brand application for a gentleman's outfitter? Although I would never expect the obvious from you, you can kind of smell the essence of the brand, can't you? When applying the brand, you can imagine how the sign up panel might look and how text style might alter to reinforce that brand. Do you get me?

Try it. How did you do?

How can I bring it all together?
The problem: to our users this website is a place that perhaps they might go to buy that special bow tie. It probably isn't a place where customers will congregate and make it a central part of their online lives, right?

We can still apply the rules we did to the other site, we can integrate a Twitter account, a Facebook profile maybe, is there anything else we could do to bring it all together? What if...

What if...
The What if... process is not a problem really; it's more of an opportunity. So, how did you get on with the What ifs for this site – did you seize the opportunity? The process should have been a lot of fun, after all you had a great brand to work with, a nice site and a free rein.

What did you do?

Here's what I came up with. What if... the site not only sold you the clobber to look sartorially elegant, but also helped you to put two and two together, taught you the correct etiquette, etc. I'm telling you I could go mad for this. We could integrate YouTube channels that teach chaps to tie a bow tie, teach them the reason the bottom button on a waistcoat should always be undone, what a pair of fishtail trousers looks like and when is the right time to wear tweed.*

What if registered users could post sartorial questions to the resident expert, the answers viewable by all (good for SEO after all) for example, "Dear Henry, I've heard in the best circles that your pocket square should not be identical to your tie, is this true?". You can perhaps see that the site might become the destination for the modern gentleman to buy, discuss and learn about the correct way one might dress. What if you could actually see what that purple set of braces looks like on a blue shirt with cream trousers? Handy if you have these sorts of concerns.

What if users could log into their accounts using Facebook?

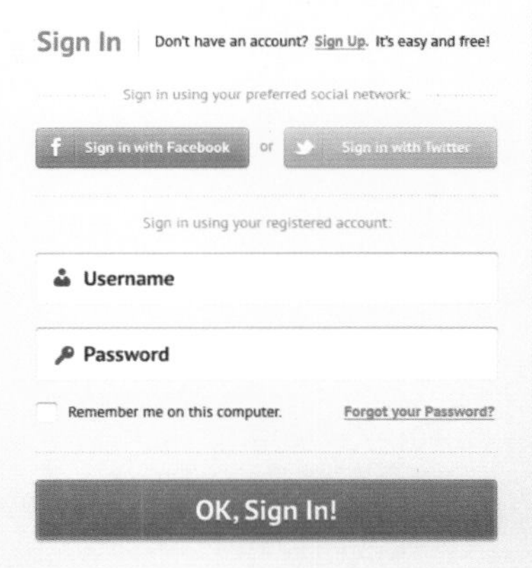

Sign up!: this interface lets you sign in using your Facebook or twitter profile. How would you redesign it so that it is sartorially elegant? Try on the notes and sketches page overleaf.

**Tweed is attire best suited to Country pursuits.*

Thinking like this will help you to separate the website from the crowd, transform you from just being a designer as well as giving your client reasons to create a brilliant site. Or you could just list bow ties for sale.

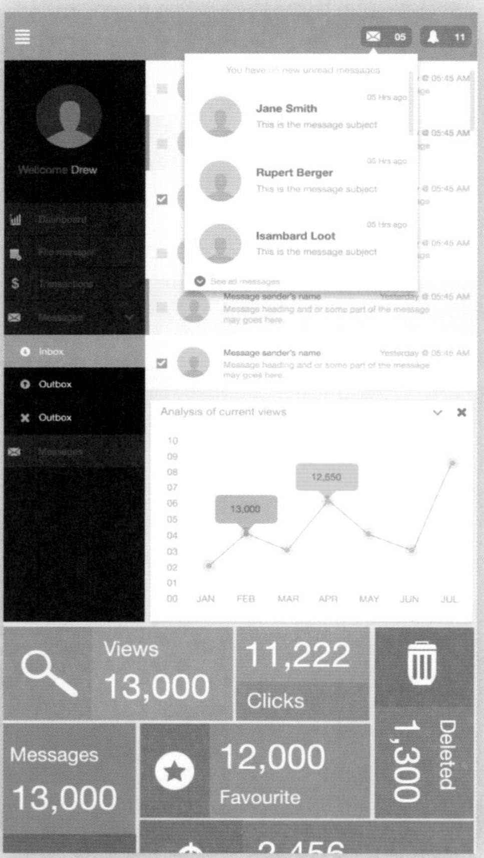

There is another type of site and interface that a designer often is asked to consider and needs careful thought before wading into the minutiae of design – any site that requires a user profile, a large amount of content, user groups or any kind of network.

This type of site (with lots of admin features) provides a whole heap of issues for the designer that affect the navigation, structure – just about everything. Under most circumstances once the user has logged in, they will arrive at a 'dashboard' of some kind. This interface allows them to edit their profiles, post content and see content that has been presented to them, etc.

Typically there can be a lot of data and functions to display, the example here shows an interface (which I have to admit I purchased as a template) with a stack of content.

Projects like social network sites, intranets or community sites have so many types of functionality and within that is a host of different scenarios.

Admin essence: I detect essence of Microsoft in this template design.

The presentation of the functionality differs from a typical website because the interface should be a graphic display of all the activities they might want to perform, a 'tool' box if you like. The scoping of the user journeys is mega important when working on these types of interfaces.

NOTES AND SKETCHES

Can you do better? How would you design a nice sign up panel? Have a go here.

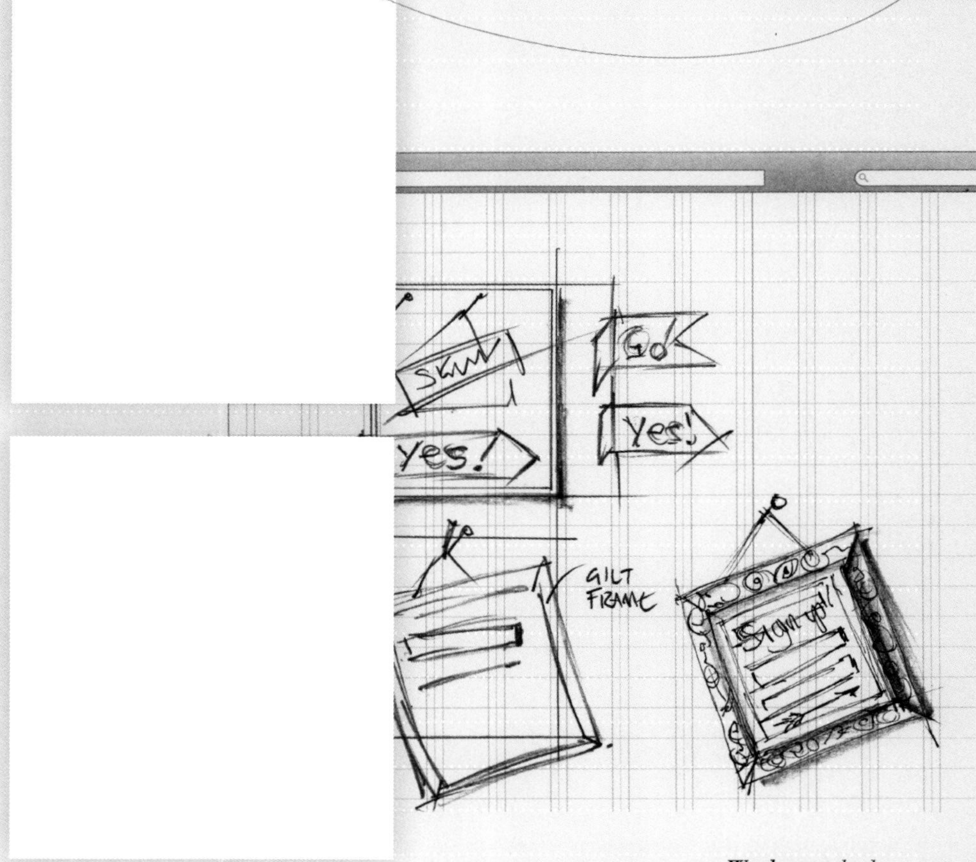

Wonky: *anybody spot what's wrong with this idea?* *Answer on page 31.*

DESIGNING

Like almost everything in life, there are conventions out there that help people understand what to do and what to expect. It will depend on your end client whether these conventions are relevant to your design or not. After all, conventions are there to be flaunted: feel free to flaunt away. But flaunting comes with a price, and no matter how left-field your client is, if people can't use the site they will leave. In this section, I point out some of the conventions that have come to underpin web design, so if you've got it, flaunt it.

Click it and take me home, more on page 129

The logo on the site should link to the home page. I can't see any circumstance why this wouldn't always be the case. Just do it.

Search bars and logins tend to be top right of the screen. People expect these types of 'utilities' to be there or thereabouts. If your site requires a login, then place it where it can be seen, but so it isn't too prominent and detracts from the overall message. Make sure that once the users are logged in the status changes to 'log out' and appears in the same place on the site. It makes life easy.

Search bars are similar; they need not dominate but be there for the people who want to use them. The positioning and prominence of any function should be determined by the way users will interact with the site. A site like Amazon needs a prominent search bar. Imagine a site like Amazon without a search!

Footers are very handy things. They are lowly areas, stuck at the bottom of the page that are obliged to house things like copyright and privacy policies. They are sleeping giants that can help users with navigation. They can also help with search engine optimisation by pointing search engines to site maps or store all (or the main) of the links in live text format. Search engines like live text, they are a bit like pandas and are only interested in consuming one thing. There has been a fashion for 'fat footers', these are not people with large shoes, but websites that really go to town and include a massive amount of links, way down at the bottom of the page.

With search engines it is live text, with Pandas it's bamboo.

Wonky answer: *there is no way of coding form fields at an angle.*

Your navigation should be the clearest thing on your site, so your user should always know what's on offer and where they are. I go about this in detail, but things like highlighting the section you are in and a rollover state is vital for keeping people comfy and happy. When an item changes state, or alters when you are just about to click on it, the user knows that something does something – if you see what I mean?

No doubt about it, this is a button.

Buttons should look like buttons. Does this need to be said? Yes. They don't have to be 3D in style and look like the front of your stereo. If you want somebody to do something, sign up, buy now or whatever, the element they click on needs to look like something to click on. This is probably the most stupid and obvious thing anybody has ever said to you. But it does have to be said. Don't make buttons look like some obscure artistic elements that users have to find and then guess if it is a button or not. Because they may not find it, they probably won't click on it and they will go elsewhere.

Make sure you know what you're doing before you start

Make sure you are clear about the brief. Read it. Read it again. If you are unsure about anything, ask the client. It will make them feel involved, clients like to be involved and a conversation with a client before you start designing will not only get things right from the start, but enable you to discuss things that perhaps they have not considered, it will help you avoid the cardinal sin, being; "I just assumed". Assume nothing, whatever you assume is likely to be wrong, because you are not sure what the client means, it may mean starting all over again. If you have to start all over again, it will be your own fault, nobody else's – because you haven't understood what the client wants. There is, of course, an exception when it is not your fault if you have to start again and that is when the client changes their mind. They do do that quite a bit. But you will, of course, have got a written brief first, and if the brief changes, then you are well within your rights to charge them extra. But you must tell them that before you start doing extra work that it will cost extra – and get them to sign the costs off before you start.

At this stage, it never hurts to have a quick word with the developers. Developers like a challenge, but they work in the realms of reality and can let you know if a certain element you would like to introduce in a certain way will make their lives very difficult.

I know, I know, you are itching to start designing.

Get designing

Before you start, make sure you have been through the *Thinking* process and got your head around what the site could do, how it could grow and what if...

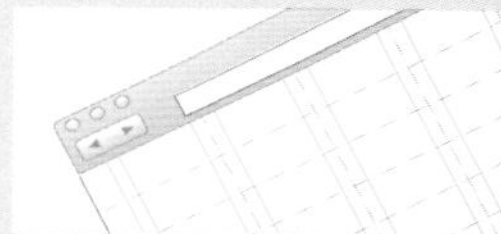

960 grid templates, jolly handy they are.

For the people out there who read my book *Know Your Onions: Graphic Design*, then you will know how much I bang on about using a pencil and paper to get your ideas out quickly. Even though web is a screen based thing, it does not matter. I don't care if you are designing a car, a shed or an arc, scribbling your ideas down on a piece of paper is the way forward.

Later you will read about using grids, mostly the 960 grid. You can buy pads with the 960 grid printed on them, or download a template from knowyouronions.info, or you can use the back of an envelope. It doesn't really matter. It does matter to push ideas around, explore possibilities and unleash your creativity, there is nothing better.

A lot of people start designing the home page first. It is a natural place to start, of course. For websites like the accountants we discussed above, there is no reason why you shouldn't start on the home page.

For bigger sites with lots of content, it is worth remembering that the home page is a culmination of all of the website's content. It's a place where clients like to highlight the main functions and content. In these instances, if you can hold off designing the home page and design some of the main content sections first. These pages will help dictate how those content pages, or the content they hold, will appear on the home page. Does that make sense? A website with a lot of content should have a home page that in some way collects and displays the entire scope of the site – a tall order indeed.

Important

OK, let's deal with both scenarios.

Home page first. You will know by now what elements are to appear on the home page. One of the main things with any site is the navigation. It's often the one element that has not been considered widely enough and can therefore cause whopping great problems later.

It may be worth your while having a look through the section about navigation in this book at this stage.

Let's assume the site will have these elements on the home page:

- A horizontal navigation bar with dropdowns for sub sections.
- Three 'entry points' for products.
- A login/logout.
- Descriptive text.
- Imagery, however that might manifest itself.
- News listing.
- A footer with a copy of the main navigation.

This keeps things nice and simple.

Sharpen your pencil and pause. You can probably see in your mind's eye how the site might pan out. That goes there, that goes there. You may even dream in colour. Your mind is a temptress. Because you, as the impetuous, young spirited and confident designer that you are, will think you can leap into Photoshop and crack on. Be my guest. But you are heading for boring, unimaginable solutions that will take you an age to get right. If you ever get it right.

So, to start, service your mistress and jot down on paper the site you have in your mind. It should take about two minutes.

Now, look again. Try something different, work on new ideas, not just putting the same elements in different places, but ideas. As a designer, your reason for being should be ideas. This process that we are going through is all about ideas and less about layout.

How can you present your client's business, the site's content, the functionality in a brilliant way? Sketch as many as you

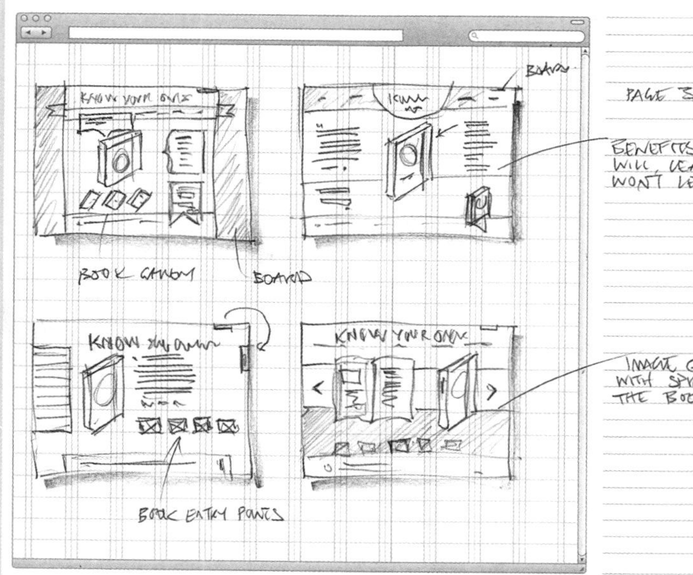

Elements in the sketches include:
Navigation
Large image
Dropdown menu
Entry points
Login/log out
Text and a quote
Carousel
Footer
Logo

can in ten minutes. It does not matter if they are all rubbish. What matters is getting your mind, your mistress, interested in the possibilities of something other than what might be expected.

By the way, I use the term 'mistress' in a non-gender specific way. 'Master' doesn't really convey what I'm trying to say. All I'm trying to say is control your urges, channel your energy into creation (this is beginning to sound like *Know Your Onions: Procreation* – which would make an excellent top-shelf publication!).

Difficult client: *of course in this instance the client is me.*

Keep at it, keep going, keep going even after you get to that stage where your mind says 'I can't think of anything else'. You can, trust me.

In my company we have a process for this, we call it the Creative Equation. It's a system for generating oodles of ideas in no time at all. If you worked for me, I'd want to see masses of ideas in an hour, that's why I gave you the job in the first place.

Creative Equation

As far as I am aware, there is no equation which shows that an increase in creativity is a direct cause of the time spent. I make this jolly clear (I hope) in *Know Your Onions: Graphic Design.*

Yes, this section is repeated, and yes if you bought the first book (thanks) you will have read all this. BUT not everybody is as forward thinking as you, and before you start moaning, it's been rewritten.

What I mean is, the longer you spend trying to think of an idea, does not necessarily mean you will come up with a good one. Some ideas come in a flash, like Archimedes in the bath, others take hours of ruminating to come up with. Coming up with lots of them requires the right conditions.

My point is this: there are ways of working that will help you and your team generate ideas quickly and collaboratively in a relatively short space of time. The final effect increases output and the likelihood of coming up with that showstopper – in *less time.*

If I give a brief to a designer without implementing any system, chances are that he or she will sit at their desk for as long as they can (weeks, if you leave them to it), developing endless ideas or infinite variations on the same idea and going off on all manner of tangents. Often the designer has lost sight of the original brief and the goals set out at the beginning. Eventually, I can bear it no longer and I call them to discuss where they have got to so far. I have, on occasions, been pleasantly surprised and the designer has come up with a solution that ticks all the boxes – but this is very rare. Most of the time, we have a conversation that starts with the designer saying, 'I don't really feel this is working. I know they are called Penguin Pens but I thought a crocodile smoking a pipe looked better.'

Even if you work on your own, if you apply this simple process, it will help you generate more ideas, develop them faster and more coherently and, with luck and effort, generate better ideas.

This is how it works. When a brief comes into our office, we have a ten-minute chat and go through the requirements with the team. We make sure we understand what the client wants, which isn't always what they need. We include everybody in this chat. Not just the designers – everybody! (Our accounts assistant came up with a name and identity for a company in an hour.) *Everybody* has good ideas.

The team then gets one hour to come up with ideas. One hour, nothing more. Use a pen and paper, not a computer, it's much, much quicker and you don't waste time thinking about which typeface to use. The idea is to stretch the brief as far as you like, no inhibitions, just pure creativity.

After an hour (no more), we have another meeting where we all take turns to talk through our ideas. There are no bad ideas – ever – and other people are encouraged to chip in with comments and suggestions. This system multiplies the creativity by the amount of people in the team; the more people (within reason), the more ideas, the more comments, the more potential. This is an equation that works: the number of ideas generated x the number of people x the creative interaction = creativity, divided by time.

$$(\text{No. of ideas} \times \text{No. of people}) \times \text{creative interaction} = \sqrt[\text{TIME}]{\text{CREATIVITY}}$$

At the second meeting, one of two things might happen; either we are all floundering and we talk over why we find it difficult and start again. It's not a problem, as we've only effectively spent an hour, so not much has been lost.

Does it add up? I'm not sure it does.

The other typical outcome is two or three ideas hit the table which are worth working up: people offer up their suggestions or a good idea comes out of a stinker (always present all the ideas in these meetings, no matter how bad).

Whatever the outcome of the first hour, the meeting ends and back to the drawing board we all go, for another hour, no more.

We then meet again. By now, it is almost certain that enough good ideas have been generated and, on most occasions, we have far too many. So the Creative Director picks out three or four of the best and someone is chosen to develop them to a higher standard. We don't have a fixed time period for this, but because the chosen person knows exactly what is needed, dealing with the mechanics of generating it on a computer doesn't take very long.

At this stage, we print them out (yes, even though they are designs for screen) and stick them on the wall. We use a really big 'tab grabber', the sort of thing they use in restaurants to hold up the orders. People then mill around making comments, rushing up to the work with black pens and bottles of liquid paper, writing or drawing their comments on the work and general chin stroking.

By the end of this process, which usually takes three to four hours, the job is done. It is a great system, it really works, people get enthused by it, clients enjoy hearing about it and the results are fantastic. After you have been through this process a few times, you never go back. The process is easier to manage if your team is more than one person (i.e. a team) but no bigger than six people.

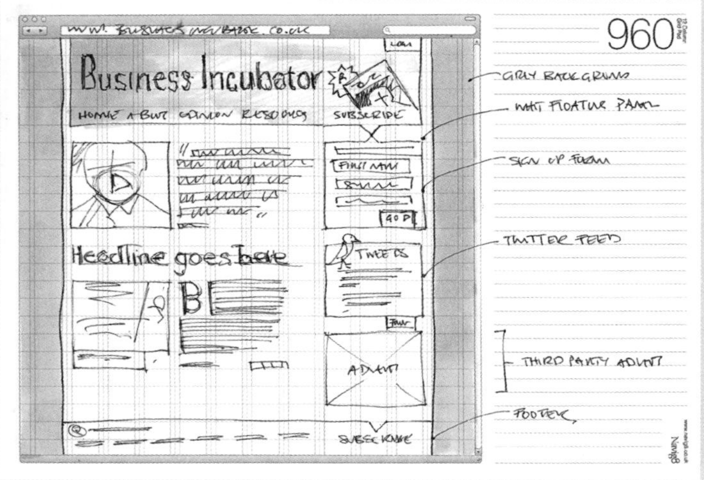

Not so rough: despite this only being a sketch it shows a tremendous level of detail enabling me to make 'deep' design decisions in a fraction of the time it would take in Photoshop.

Don't forget to play to people's strengths; don't get your best typographer to work up the illustrative concept, even if he or she came up with the idea.

By now, you should have lots of sketches and lots of ideas.

Go through them, either on your own or with your Creative Director. Select the ones that light your fire. Are you sure they are still appropriate? Remember, people will still need to understand how to navigate through the site and find what they are looking for. Choose a few, say three to five.

Now, go back to your pad, and this is a good time to work on a 960 pad if you have one, but if you don't, no matter. Redraw your concepts. Focus on the detail a bit more and as you draw the elements that will appear on the screen, visualise them. Draw them to a much higher degree. Use the same mind's eye that tried to distract you earlier (or your mistress) to help you start to think about the type of image you would like there, how big that piece of text might be, what colour would make that panel look great. If it helps, scribble some notes in the margin. But don't stray away from a pencil and paper just yet. It's OK to use a pen if you like.

After this round of development, things are shaping up, in your mind and on paper. This whole process may seem like you are slowing things down. I promise that you will reap the benefits in spades.

Time to review these designs again, you may find that perhaps three out of your five look like an award-winning site, maybe more, maybe less. If you are not sure about one, either ditch it or try to solve the problems at this stage, on paper, before moving on. Don't begin to think you can fix what is wrong when working up your designs in Photoshop. You won't, you'll just mess around and waste time. Go back to the pen and paper. The first fifty times you do this, it will probably drive you bonkers. But in time, it's like composing a symphony, the design flows on to the page; the more you do it, the faster you become. The faster you become, the more time you have to be creative – the better your design work.

I would like to point out that I have not composed a symphony as yet. If anybody out there wants to write *Know Your Onions: Composing a Symphony,* do let me know.

By now it probably feels like a long journey, if you have the sketches and the preparation done you are ready to create a masterpiece. After all, Scott of the Antarctic didn't wake up one morning, give Oates a buzz and say, "I fancy a stroll in the snow, wanna come? Bring a flag, old man and perhaps

Robert Falcon Scott

some biscuits." Preparation, preparation, preparation – as bank robbers say.

Fire up the application you want to use to design your website in. These days you can use most programmes, some lend themselves to the job better than others.

Try to follow your sketches as closely as you can, and do not deviate from them, even as you go through the layout process and realise that things aren't quite as they should be, it doesn't matter at this stage. As I mentioned earlier this stage is the best investment in your design process ever, and you only get this one chance.

Open up a new 'page' as it is easier if you are working in a pixel based application, because pixels are what make up our screens. At the moment, who knows what will happen in the future, web pages could be made up of neutrons, but for now, it's pixels. Now open your application, take a deep breath and focus on taking your sketches to infinity, and beyond!

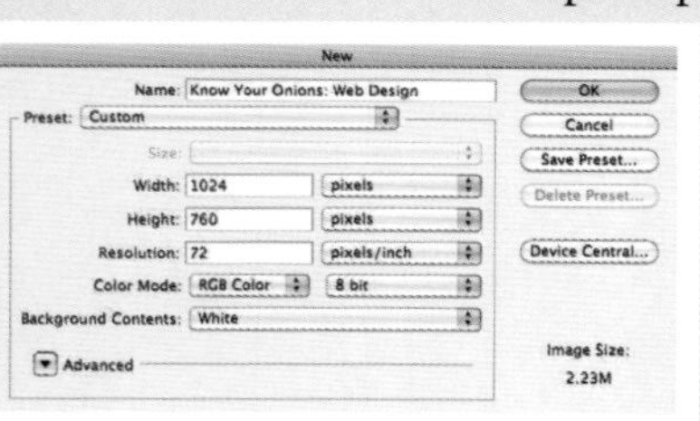

A nice shiny new Photoshop document...

In the old days, we had to work with a size of 800 x 600 pixels or less because we worked on computers made of plaster and wood. These old computers were very fragile, often made by IBM, which stands for 'I Broke Mine'. Now the screen resolution for browsers and screens (and that does not include other devices) is much bigger, at the moment 1024 x 768 pixels for monitors and sometimes more besides.

Design the page as you view it. That means that you need to view the pages at the true pixel size it will be seen at. Most applications will show you this by per cent – 100%. Design the page as it will be seen. This is mega important. If you design a website in illustrator, twice the size, every graphic you produce will be compromised and look awful when it is turned into glorious HTML or shiny graphics. So, let's say you are in Photoshop, make sure your page view is at 100% at 72ppi, set up to be 1024 x 768 pixels. The PPI stands for Pixels Per Inch. This resolution does not apply to everything, mind, but it is the right resolution for computer monitors.

Have I told you about templates? I'm not sure. I'm writing this looking over Lake Garda, so my mind may not be with you, it's looking over the lake in the warm summer evening. Aside from the 960 grid, you should begin to start to store templates that help you take your sketches into an application and make them 'pixel perfect'. I learnt the phrase from an ex-employee of mine, called Lee Suttey. He was pixel perfect and could tell looking at a Photoshop document, if anything was not aligned correctly, by one pixel. His hair was a mess mind, but hey.

Once you design a few websites, be sure to keep all the files close to you, keep them filed so that you can refer back. I have a folder called 'web pages templates' that I often refer to, silly name I know, it should have been called 'Julie'. When you get things like the masthead depth right, or the associated content right when working on a particular project, it makes life easier next time around if you look at these templates and let them inform your next design project that needs a masthead. Wait. I am not saying that one design fits all. Why would I? I've just asked you to go through the process of being creative and coming up with new ideas. What I am saying is, when working on a website that may need associated content, news, Tweets and other stuff in a 1024 screen width. If you have a template where you have got it right, keep it, it's handy. No point re-inventing the wheel, that's all.

I suggest you keep a folder with files that have been through the mill, come out of the other side and have probably been built and used. So that you know this stuff works.

Let's get on with it, shall we?

I'll assume you have the company logo and a few brand elements to start the process off. Remember, we are working on Project One, an accountant's website. You will have your brief and what-not.

The first thing I suggest you do is start a resource folder. It is a folder with 'things' that may help you bring the site design together. Remember, you can't knick stuff from the internet. You have to find appropriate images and illustrations that either you have paid for, or are free. That's not an 'I'll get away with it' moment. You are a professional, with a professional client and all hell will break loose if you knick an image from some litigious fellow. They will find out. So don't do it. Don't even include them in the pitch, if you put images into a pitch that you cannot legally use and the client approves them, then you are stuffed.

If you can't find the images that you are looking for, put in a place-holder, but make sure you tell the client that is a place-holder, write it over the image if you have too. Using royalty free images can be very creative. It still works, it just takes a bit of experience to get it right.

Once you build up your assets (assets are the things you need to use to visualise your design) you can start to place them on the page.

If you have worked through the Creative Equation, you will know that you can share the assets from the resource folder and move towards a salient concept very quickly.

Look at your sketches and start to bring your assets into the page. Place them. Don't dump them. Spend a few moments looking at how they sit on the page and before you let them drop, make sure they sit 'right'. This is layout. Slow yourself right down, take your time. The slower you are, the faster you will be, if you see what I mean?

This is not creative. Creative came before this. This is only taking an idea, your idea, and laying it out. Slow down. Better to place and be exact than charge about throwing things on the page – that was done in the sketching stage, right?

Learning to sketch well is a skill in itself, it will take time and practice, but once you can do it, you'll be set for the rest of your life.

Your job now is to lay out the pages, perhaps three home pages, as you have designed them, as your vision, as you saw it in your mind's eye.

Be precise. Even if it ain't right. Try to follow your sketch exactly. The more you do this, the more care you take with your sketches, the faster you will be, the more time you will have to be creative. I know it is hard and I know I'm repeating myself. I know it's hard because I train my staff to do it, but my staff – when they get it right – are the fastest, most creative bods you'll find.

I can't teach you to be creative. You either are, or you are not. Even if you are just a little creative and not a creative genius, I can teach you a system to maximise your creativity and time, in fact, I just have.

You have now been through the first step, the best bit really. So now we move on to laying out your work, creating your graphics and tackling those tricky design problems.

Copyright

It is very easy to get carried away on the internet and search for images for your designs and stuff them in willy nilly. Just because it is on the internet does not mean it is free to use. Sure, there is lots of free stuff that you can use, but you need to be sure first. Wikicommons offers some material that is free, so do other sites, but check the licensing. You may think you won't get caught, but if you do, you could be in a whole heap of trouble.

You can use stock images as placeholders, but you must explain this to your client and all of them will need to be sourced and purchased. You can buy and download graphics and use them, but don't knick anything. Your work is copyrighted and so is other people's.

Wikimedia Commons: You get what you pay for, but some of the stuff on this site and others like it can be useful.

Note the licensing terms, these clearly state what you can use the asset for and what you can't.

There are lots of other free sites out there, and of course, lots of royalty free image libraries.

WORKING

Project management

Even if you work in a vast corporate design group, with members of staff whose role is to cover every conceivable activity, from ordering the paper clips, to selecting the pastries, you will still have to project manage to a certain extent. If you work for yourself, it's up to you to buy the paper clips and you probably won't have the time or the money to buy pastries.

PMs: a good PM is jolly organised and very pro-active. They like GANT charts, schedules and highlighter pens.

Project management covers a few key areas for most designers:
- Timing and scheduling.
- Managing expectations.
- Dealing and coordinating clients, suppliers and the development team.
- Scoping (sometimes) and managing changes to the scope.

There are other things like estimating and invoicing that go into the project management pot, but to go into these in detail would detract from the purpose of this book.

If, per chance you, have read *Know Your Onions: Graphic Design*, some of this will be familiar to you. It never hurts to be as good at design as you are at managing your work.

Timing and scheduling

Things always take longer than you expect, guaranteed. Missing a deadline should be a mortal sin in your mind. Designers are often blasé about deadlines, but clients aren't. Don't miss deadlines. Allow enough time to do the job and then add on a third.

When a brief comes in, take a long hard look at it. The client will usually tell you when they require the final product, so work out how long it will take – work backwards. Even if you can knock it off in an afternoon, don't send it over until the work is due, or just before. You only make things difficult for yourself later if you send work in before it is required.

Good project management, filing and scheduling is even more important for web design than it is for print design. Expect it to take a good 20–30 per cent of the time spent on any one project.

When a brief comes in, even if the job isn't due for weeks, look through the files *straightaway.* If something is missing, corrupted or you don't understand an instruction, then you can get it cleared up immediately. This not only looks good, it is good.

File things properly, there is more about this in 'File management'.

During the course of a project, there will be key stages, or milestones. Often you can stave off an eager client by giving them things piecemeal. Do what is important to them first, not what you fancy doing the most.

Take responsibility for the project yourself. You should never rely on the client. I have heard designers say things like 'well, I wasn't sure what you wanted to do about that', or 'I haven't heard from you so…'. If you haven't heard from them, chase them up, if you don't know what they mean or want, ask. Clients like being involved in the process and like being consulted, most would love to be graphic designers themselves.

The more proactive, organised and efficient you are, the better job you will do. The more hassle you take away from the client and the easier you make their lives, the more they will want to commission you, and you will become their favoured supplier.

Managing expectations

Clients get annoyed when you say Wednesday and they get it Thursday. But there is more to managing expectations than hitting deadlines. After you have had your brainstorm, you have come up with loads of ideas and worked a few of them up – then you are ready to present.

Always be one step ahead and make sure you are ready before the deadline. If you think you can rustle up a home page and a sub-page in two days, double it. It always takes longer than you think. Clients also take longer than they think, so this presents a tricky problem when you work on your schedule, you'll see why overleaf.

File management

I know this is boring, but good file management makes a HUGE difference if you get it right. It will save you time, you will be happier and live longer. It never ceases to astonish me, even in the biggest agencies, that there isn't a fixed file structure for jobs. The amount of times I have seen designers lose jobs, save files on other people's machines across networks or give them inappropriate names is amazing.

Copy this folder structure onto your machine and use it for every job you do. It was 'designed' for print jobs, but with a bit of tweaking it can be used for any sort of job – websites, packaging, you name it. You can download a folder structure from the website: www.knowyouronions.info.

The folder structure is fairly self-explanatory, and the way I tested it is, if another designer goes onto your computer, they should be able to locate the most up-to-date file, the right images and text immediately. I can't tell you how important this is; if you don't get into the habit of managing your files and versions, you will waste oodles of time, which you could spend designing or drinking gin and tonics.

When I do a job for a client, I give it a version number and a sensible name. like 'ABC_Client-Homepage-01.psd', but you have to watch out, because the names can get a bit long. The important bit is the job description and version number. Every time I do a set of revisions, or a major change to a job, I always 'save as' and increase the version number. This is a good idea, because occasionally you might need to go back to an earlier version; it also helps you track the number of revisions you have done for the client and they can see the number of versions as well.

When you email over the business card PDF and its version number is 18, the client might start thinking about the number of changes they are making and consider the time and money being wasted making revisions – maybe. When you get approval, that approval is attached to that file version. So, 'save as' for the very last time and change the version number to 'AW', which stands for 'artwork'. This completely removes the guesswork forever.

There is no artwork: for web design 'artwork' isn't really the case because the code is the artwork and that is ever changing, but AW is a good signifier for a final file.

Also, as text is supplied from the client during the project, it can get confusing when clients call their files 'FinalVersionToUse.doc' and then send you another file later on called, 'UseThisOne.doc'. When text comes in, rename the file supplied to something like 'home-text_01.doc', then if another version comes in, name that 'home-text_02.doc', it doesn't take a genius.

Text
Kayleigh-proofing queries.docx
Know Your Onions ...esign-02-Back.doc
Know Your Onions Web design-03.doc
Know Your Onions Web design-04.doc
Know Your Onions Web design-05.doc
Know Your Onions Web design-07.doc
Know Your Onions Web design-08.doc
Know Your Onions Web design-08a.doc
Know Your Onions Web design-08b.doc
Know Your Onions Web design-09.doc
Know Your Onions Web design-09a.doc
Know Your Onions Web design-09b.doc
Know Your Onions Web design-09c.doc
Know Your Onions Web design-10a.doc
Know Your Onions Web design-11.doc

Smug: I definitely know which version is the latest here.

A lot of applications these days will automatically add the applications affix (i.e. .qxd for Quark or .indd for InDesign, .psd for Photoshop), but if not, it can be helpful in identifying a file's application.

Good file naming helps on so many levels. For instance, if I'm searching an archive disk, I can search using the client name, job type or the affix 'aw.indd', etc.

A word on approval; if you have emailed, posted, or even faxed (faxed if you still live in a cave) a proof to a client and everything is done and dusted, you need to get approval. Get it in writing. This helps clients 'focus the mind', it helps them realise that the responsibility for content is down to them (it is, of course). The best way is to have an approval disclaimer at the bottom of your email. With the JPEG attached, with its version number, the client can reply to that email with 'approved' in the subject or in the body of the email.

File the email in the administration folder. That way you have a record of the written sign-off and you can wave it in front of the client if they missed something.

That's digital file management, but you will also need a place to keep all the bits of paper that come with a project. You need a 'Job Bag'. This can be an expensive agency folder, a plastic pocket or a C4 manila envelope, it doesn't matter. Bung all your printer's quotes, your estimates, notes from clients and most recent proofs in there.

I had a stack printed (very cheaply) with boxes for me to record important things about a job. There is nothing more helpful than when a client rings up for a reprint a year later, if you can pull out the Job Bag, ring the right printer, quote them their reference (and check the costs) and order the job in seconds.

If you are working for an agency, they will want you to record your time. It is vital to keep a track of how long you spend on things. We use job sheets at Navig8, that way I can see who has done what, for how long and what to charge the client.

To gather up all of these file management elements, i.e. Folder Structure, Job Bag and Job Sheet – we use a job number. It is the unique identifier that ties all of the elements together and goes on the invoice.

It's a system, it works. You can buy file management and project management software, I think you can even use a web interface, but the system described above can be used by anyone, big or small, and it's free.

It's urgent!

I can understand surgery being urgent, I can see the need for calling out an electrician in an emergency – but it still amazes me that any sort of graphic design can ever be urgent. But it is. It always is.

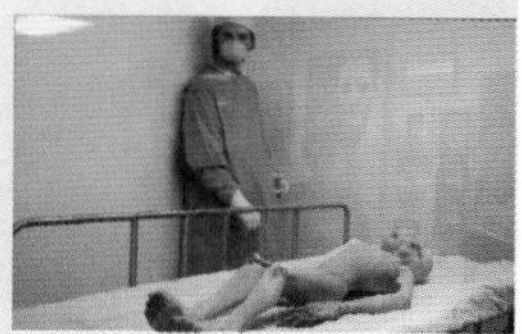

***Aliens:** they have design needs as well y'know.*

Can you imagine any possible scenario where graphic design is really, really urgent? "Mr. President, the alien crafts are only three hours away from entering the earth's atmosphere. We need an HTML email with "We come in peace" designing and we need it now!".

I would say a good 25 per cent of our work is deemed by the client to be 'urgent'. There is only one reason for this, as far as I can work out over my 25 years plus' experience; no planning. You can guarantee that the person commissioning the design work has a boss, and that boss has a boss, and that person forgot to commission the poster in good time, when the aliens were spotted just left of Pluto, and now it's down to you to get it sorted.

The point is that you have to deal with the situation. You have to turn this 'urgency' into something that will benefit you and the client.

Different companies deal with urgent jobs in different ways. Some just say 'no'. They risk the financial reward and acclaim of being the first agency to communicate with aliens. Others say, 'OK, but it will cost extra', and very few clients like paying extra. Some just say 'yes', no matter the situation and put themselves at risk of doing poor work and producing HTML emails with errors in them that say, 'We come in pieces' instead of "We come in peace".

OK, enough of the alien stuff. There is a middle ground. You know how long things really take, you know when you can turn it around a bit faster whilst still doing a good job. You should also know the factors that are out of your control that will make you miss your deadline.

Can you actually do it in time? Bearing in mind what you know, add a few hours/days to your timescale, you'll need it. Can you still do it in time? If you can't do the job in time, tell them straightaway and tell them why. Better to say no and lose the job than fail trying. But if you can do it, I make the following suggestions.

Firstly, tell your client that if you can do it, you will. But make sure you tell them you are helping them out; if you don't do that, they will think you can do it every time.

Next, point out the steps in the process that could jeopardise the delivery date. If you don't know already, these include:

- Client not approving costs.
- Client not supplying material, or supplying material in a format you can't use.
- Client changing their mind.
- Client making endless last-minute amends.
- Natural disaster or invasion of extra-terrestrials (couldn't resist).

There are ways and means of saying things. If you outline your response, as I have above, you will put their nose out

Dear Isambard,

The deadline is exceedingly tight, but I can see the reason for the urgency and I'll do what I can to help.

I will have to put my other projects on hold – I can't promise I will always be able to drop everything in the future.

I've quickly outlined the process with timings, which we will need to meet in order for us to hit your deadline. Do you think you will be able to achieve this from your side?

Today: Approving costs and timings

Day X: You to supply all text in final form and images as high-resolution digital files and a short brief, outlining your requirements.

Day X: Concepts and first proof presented as a static visual(s)
Day X: Comments and amendments
Day X: Second proof of chosen concept
Day X: Final comments and sign-off ready for build
Day X: Test link
Day X: Functionality testing and bug fixing
Day X: Development and final platform test
Day X: Final test link
Day X: Written approval
Day X: Deploy to live server
[You will need to add in the estimate here.]

If you would like to proceed, please send me your order, agreement of costs and timings, and I will start straightaway.

of joint (that was just between you and me). To 'put a doily under it', as they say, try something like this (above).

You should be able to see what I'm doing here. It makes things very, very clear. It is helpful, it is proactive and it covers your arse to some extent. The client will definitely miss their deadlines. But you will have allowed for that in your schedule and you will be able to deliver anyway. Right?

Deadlines and process: *the above example is not detailed enough for a significant web project, but it is a start.*

Follow this route and even though the client didn't honour their side of the bargain, you will be a hero and the Earth will be saved. Say 'yes' to something you can't achieve – and even if you do your best and fail – you will be to blame.

File formats

File formats are very important to computers. They like to know what is what and they do this by looking at the file affix. The affixes are the characters that come after the full stop (or period if you are in the good old U S of A). Most of the time designers couldn't care less, but as I say, computers get uppity if you give them the wrong file types.

Below (right) is a list of file types that you may come across in your work and I'll give you an outline of the best applications to use when generating your work. I have not included them all, but concentrated on what I consider to be the professional designers' suite of applications and the developers' final files.

It's a bit dull, but it may come in handy when you are sitting there in a meeting and somebody starts talking about data and MySql and you don't start thinking that they mean it is their SQL and nobody else's. You seriously don't need to know what the letters stand for, but I've told you so you can show off to your friends at dinner parties, but it won't make you interesting.

MAKE SURE YOU CAN MANAGE:

- Allow enough production time and plan for the worst.
- Always add a day on to the delivery date. Allow for holidays and weekends.
- Be proactive and take the responsibility yourself.
- Manage client's expectations.
- Watch out for urgent jobs, they'll blame you in the end.

HTML: Hypertext Markup Language is the code that makes up most web pages, it creates the framework.

XML: Extensible Markup Language
A language used for storing and moving data about.

CSS: Cascading Style Sheets
This is the file that holds the styling for the elements on the page.

PHP: Hypertext Preprocessor
This script creates the functionality on the server making things 'dynamic'.

SQL: Structured Query Language
A language used for handling data.

MSQL: Mini Structured Query Language The world's most popular database language.

ASP/ASP.NET: Active Server Pages
This is Microsoft's answer to PHP.

JS: JavaScript
This language makes things happen, developers use it to make websites and widgets function.

TXT: This is a lowly text file.

PSD: Photoshop Document

PDF: Portable Document Format
These days a whole host of files can be exported and shared using this very flexible format from Adobe.

JPEG or **JPG:** Joint Photographic Expert Group
Created by a bunch of chaps who wanted a standard to compress images.

PNG: Portable Network Graphics
A compression format for images, the good thing about this format is you can use transparent backgrounds.

AVI: Audio Video Interleave
This is a video format courtesy of Microsoft.

MOV: Guess what it stands for, a video format, like mp4.

MP4: or **MPEG4**
Video format.

FLA: This is the native Flash format.

FLV: Flash Video
You guessed it, it's a Flash video format.

AI: Adobe Illustrator
This is the native file format for Illustrator files.

FHD: FreeHand Document
This is the native file format for Freehand.

There are, of course, loads of files that in the developer world, are important, but you shouldn't worry your head about them. I never have. A basic understanding will suffice. If I've missed some and you've spotted it, then that's good too.

Photoshop: image editing, obviously, but excellent for website design

Illustrator: this application is primarily vector based, so good for logos

InDesign: the master of design for print and publishing

Dreamweaver: this is as designer-friendly web build and development application

What app to use and when

Most of the time, but not all of the time, mind, the files you produce when designing web pages will be pixel based. We already know that the resolution to work in is 72 PPI. There are a few very good pixel based applications out there, some of which are free, you just need to search for them. But it has to be said that the absolute, undisputed champion is Photoshop. If you want to be a web designer, learn Photoshop.

All our web pages start their life in Photoshop. We load in a template, view it at 100% at 72 PPI and a screen size of 1024 x 768 pixels (that's four times I've told you now).

I do not work for Photoshop, I am not sponsored by them, Adobe have not offered to buy me an Aston Martin Vantage in British Racing Green with a cream leather interior. Ahem.

Photoshop has all the tools a designer needs to design beautiful web pages, set them up to make your developer happy and compress the file to its smallest size to keep your web pages lean. I'm not going to write a manual for you, do a course, experiment, learn from your colleagues.

There are a few key features that the application has. I'm well aware that other applications have similar functions, it's up to you. An Aston would be nice...

You can set up your document so that it can be 'sliced' automatically. Slicing is essentially chopping out the graphics needed to make up your design. You can set your document up so that the slices can be exported in one go.

You can also export your design or any image, to be compressed and ready for web. Let's say you have a picture of an Aston Martin for your new website, once you have cropped and scaled it as you want it, you can save for web and Photoshop will give you a preview of the effect of the image when compressed. You can adjust the compression to achieve the smallest file size possible, with acceptable image quality. Note, I said 'acceptable'. Image quality is not as important as file size in the world of the web.

Illustrator or Freehand are primarily vector based applications. They are ideally suited for drawing up illustrations, logos and things that may need to be scaled up without losing quality. There is nothing to stop you using either to design your website; it's what you feel most comfortable with. They will let you work in layers and export your files in a host of formats. Some will even let you export whole pages in HTML. I have to say, I have never done this, I've always worked with a developer to build my websites.

The controversial application is Flash. Flash does things that no other application can do, or at least not as well. But the mood has moved away from Flash. There are a few reasons for this. Flash requires a browser plugin and is not supported by iPads and iPhones. These devices rang the death knell for Flash. We'll have to see what happens next, things change. HTML 5 and JavaScript are developing to fill the gap. So what's so great about Flash?

This will keep you entertained while you wait for your Flash to load.

Flash is the master of animation and a very, very powerful tool. Whole sites can be built in Flash, you can often tell when you've hit one, because you will see a loading loop, a little clock, or graphic that tells you the file is loading.

Overly animated sites gained a reputation and a sneering response, the term being 'Flasterbation'.

Flash handles video well and it's brilliant at interactivity using timelines and movie clips. In the old days, which is about five years ago, CD ROMs were mastered by Flash.

If you want to build a website and don't want to get your hands dirty in code, Dreamweaver will do the trick. But the reality is if you want it to work properly, you have to learn a bit of code.

Most of the developers I have worked with use the most basic programmes to create code. I'm talking Notepad here. It's like watching *The Matrix* when you see them typing it in. I worked with one developer who could look at a colour and write the Hexadecimal code to match it. Freak.

Consistency

Consistency is vital to the delivery of good design. If you take a look at all the major brands, love 'em or hate 'em, they consistently apply their brand and the styles that go with it. Take a look at a big news website and the styles site-wide are consistent.

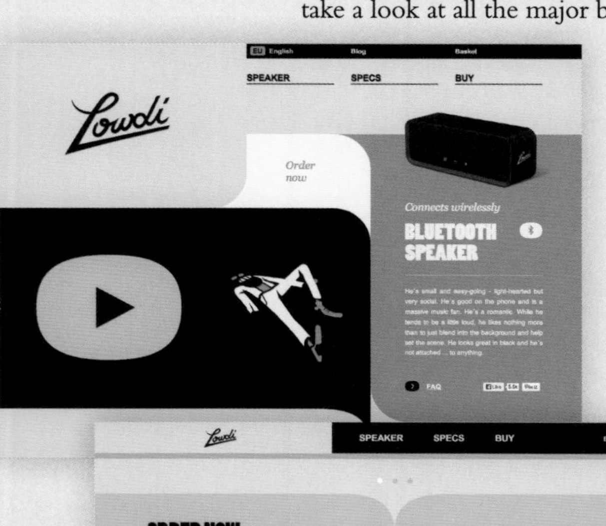

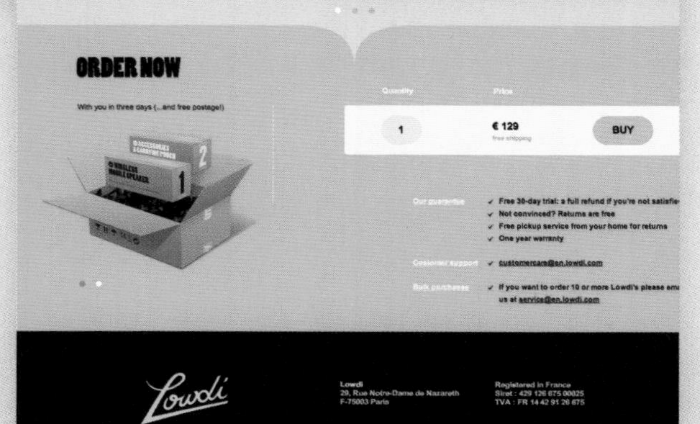

Lowdi's website only has a few styles, but the way they are mixed up and consistently applied delivers a great finish.

Here's the thing, there aren't many styles that you need. In fact, the less the better. A good headline style, subhead, body text and link style will cover a large proportion of the styles needed in any website, look at Wikipedia. Most pages have four styles. I believe consistency is one of the most important aspects of good interactive design. Make sure your styles do what they need to do to cover your content and that you implement them consistently.

If you and the information architect have done your jobs properly, the main site navigation should be consistent across the whole site. If not, why not? As a user, I want to know and see that the sections in the navigation are the same site-wide and that navigation helps me to understand how I access the content I want.

The link styles and colours should always be the same. There should be no thoughts in your mind that go, "Well, I thought this link was a bit different to the others, so I made it pink." If that even pops into your head, go and stand in the corner and think about why you haven't allowed for enough and the right styles site-wide. If your styles have been applied consistently, then the user will know what is a link, change it here and there and they will have to start thinking "Is that a link or is that pink thing something else?"

If you have a flat or 2D graphic on your site, there better be a jolly good reason why you start introducing a 3D style button. Stick to the interface design, don't start chucking 3D buttons and shadows on items when the rest of the interface is 'flat'. It just makes for a poor and inconsistent user experience. Bad for brand, bad for you and bad for them.

I can't imagine what tomfoolery people must get up to when they change what a footer looks like.

In my opinion, the only time it is acceptable to change the nature and consistency of a website interface is when the very nature of the site and its function change. An example of what that might be an embedded game or presentation perhaps. Even then, consistent use of font and colours and branding should apply.

Got it? I think I've been consistent in what I'm saying – wouldn't you agree?

Templates and elements pages

Templates are time saving and if used well, will save you the arduous part of setting up a job and applying your design. Templates do not mean every site will look the same. We have templates to start our print projects off, and one A4 leaflet never looks the same as the next, even though most start from a template.

When I talk about templates, I do not mean go and buy a website template from a website template company. These

Below: the pink bands denote the 960 grid using a 12 column grid, the guides are for the gutters between columns.

sorts of templates are for people who just want to dump some content into something that looks OK because they can't design. The templates will never, ever fit the scope of the site you are designing, how could they? That would mean that the template designer allowed for your client's needs and understood your design vision, before the project was even conceived!

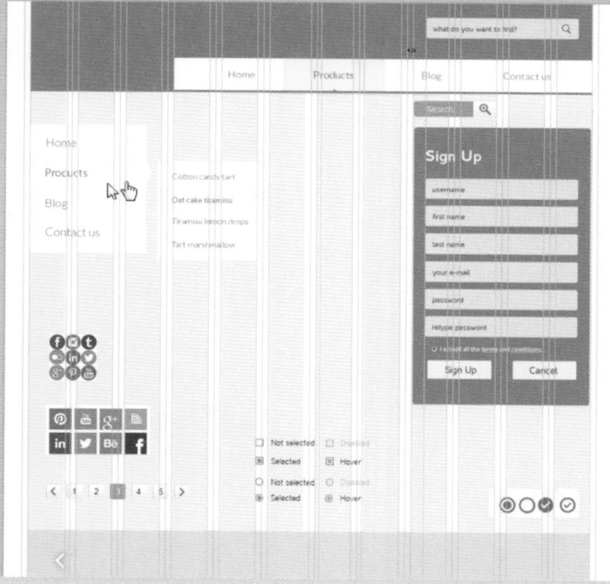

The grid templates are part of the designer's suite of templates. Over time, you should grow your set to cover the different types of sites you design.

We use a few templates that include common elements, set out on layers that can be opened up, saved as a new version – they are a brilliant starting point, but that is all they are. They might contain a few form elements for instance and these can save you time whenever you need to make a sign up form.

We talked earlier about the different types of layout, remember? It is a good idea to have these set up as templates, you won't save a massive amount of time but you will save a bit. If you are too lazy to create your own templates, then you are in a fine position as a purchaser of this book. If you register on knowyouronions.info there are some free templates you can download as a starting point.

I realise this is a bit of a mess, but it is the beginnings of my 'flat' template. I used to draw up arrows every single time I needed one, now I drag and drop.

You can put anything you like in your templates, but a set usually contains a header panel, navigation panels, footers and a few other bits and bobs.

Form elements

Forms can be styled using CSS to look any way you like. But they never look the same from browser to browser, even when they are styled. If the form elements are not styled, then each browser has a default style (see page 145) for each element and they vary with each operating system and version as well.

The illustration right shows a small selection of form elements that are typically used and styled to bring them on brand. I recommend you speak with the developer before customising the form elements too much, it can create stacks of work.

It should go without saying that if you are in a position where you are working for one particular client and over time you are being asked to visualise and design different pages and elements, then keeping a base template, with all their common elements nice and clean and ready to go, is a must. This brings us to elements pages.

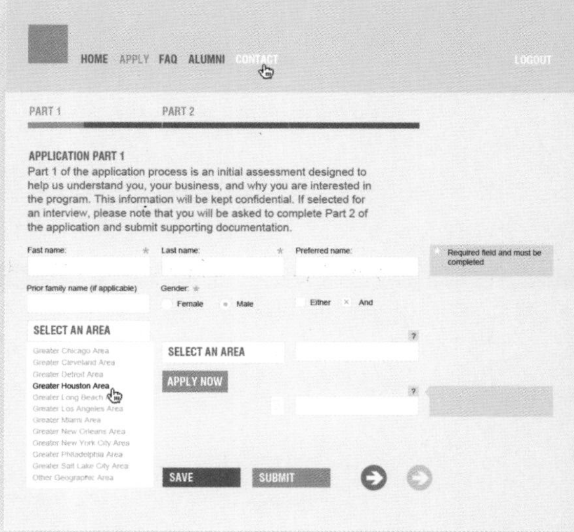

On form: *the simple palette, standard font sizes and grey background create a nice clean form.*

Elements page

I'm not sure why this happens, but in my experience, designers find it hard to get their head around an elements page, or at least they will avoid doing them. I don't know why, perhaps you can tell me, but I suspect it is because an elements page doesn't really exist.

When I say that it doesn't really exist, I'm not saying that it is in another dimension and only people who have the 'gift' can see it. I mean it is a page that will never be rendered other than to show all the common elements on the site as a visual to help the developer see and understand all the likely styles within a website.

An elements page contains every element that will be applied site wide. Some of these things are styles controlled by the basic CSS styles, some will be your own custom graphics and buttons. There is no set list of elements to include, and each site will have a different elements page. Elements pages are mega-handy templates, because if you can be bothered to set one up in the early stages of your web design project, you can quickly pull off all the elements needed for any particular page.

Below is an elements page for a website labelled so that you can see what each bit does, but as I say, each site will be different and require different elements. You can rob this one off our website as well.

Standard CSS styles should be included in your elements page. These are the standard styles that browsers recognise and search engines prioritise on a website.

H1: Main headline style
H2: Headline style
H3: Subhead style
H4: Style
Body text
Bullets list
Numbered list
Link style:
  Rollover link style
  Visited link style

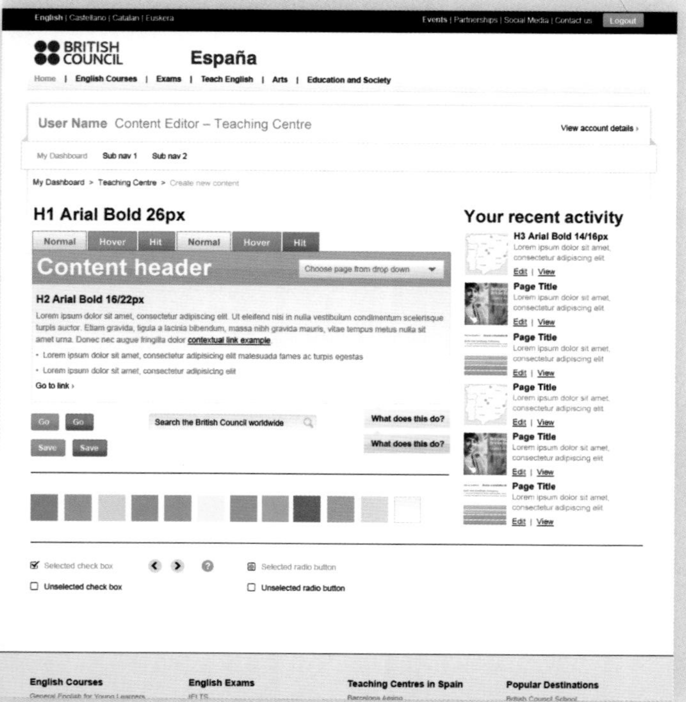

In reality this page will never exist, but you can see, in one file, all of the common styling elements that can be applied site-wide. Designing and supplying one of these saves a lot of work and uncertainty.

Marking up your PSDs

I've already told you that websites will render slightly differently on different browsers. I'll keep telling you as well. Once your design has been finalised in, say, Photoshop, the best way to get close to exactly what you want is to mark up your designs properly.

The way to do this is to create a new folder in the layers palette, and call it 'Mark up'. You can, of course, call it 'Henry'. Create a layer for your guides, we tend to use a 1 pixel line, the finest you can use and colour it a bright colour, magenta or cyan. We label everything that needs to be labelled. This makes developers very happy.

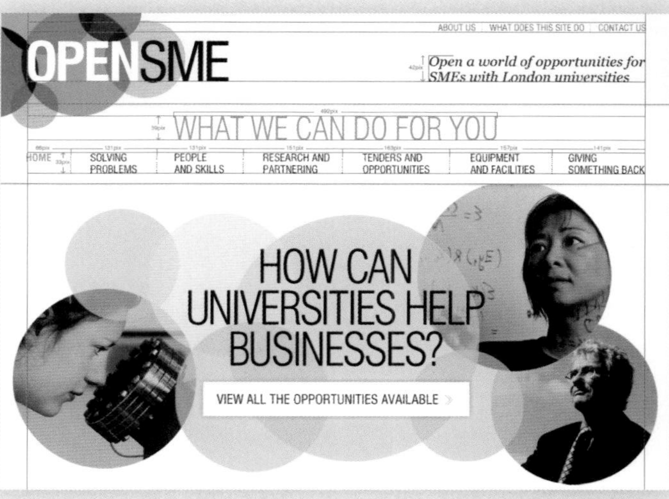

Mark up: a marked up PSD getting ready for the development stage.

The Bento box analogy applies here (see page 83). If your website design incorporates a sign up panel, then you can supply a marked up visual just for that item, and the developer will style the element, you only need to supply the element once.

Assuming that you have applied your design consistently this isn't as much hassle as it looks. If you haven't applied the style and the design consistently, then you run the risk of all your margins being different and more besides. Like everybody, some people have an eye for detail and some don't. As a designer, you should have a keen eye for detail. As I've said before, don't expect your developer to worry about such trifles as a pixel here and a pixel there – he's too busy thinking about how to make it work. Take a look at developers' own websites, they look like they were styled using a calculator.

I've included a marked up page here, and you can get it from you-know-where.

Working with the developers

Without a developer your website is just a picture. Without them, there is no web page. Whether your agency has a team of developers, or just one, or if you are using a freelancer, it makes no difference. Make sure you consult them as you go along. It is vital for you to try and understand what the build implications of your ideas will be. Just about anything can be built these days and most developers will try to accommodate what you want. You need to chat through with them what you want and how you want things to work – they will need a proper spec, which we will come to later.

Developers work in time – how long it will take for them to build what you want. The next thing I'm going to say is said with the greatest respect, but as a designer, you do need to understand that a developer will say it will take, say, eight hours to build one bit of functionality. Maybe. Those eight hours are usually longer and when you get the first test link, you shouldn't expect it to be working perfectly and looking exactly as you want it. Life just isn't like that. A lot of the time, the developer has to work out how to do something, and then try it out. Then there might be a bug that affects another bit of code and that's not even mentioning browser compatibility, which can cause a world of hurt.

The gist of all this is a change in your mindset. Interactive design isn't like print, there are too many factors that can effect things, particularly time. This is the main reason that project management and managing client expectation is vital if you want a happy team and a happy client.

Assume more work will be needed after the first test link is sent to you, assume you will need to test things before they go to the client, read the section in this book about project management. Be ready to do more.

Assume nothing

One of the best ways to ensure you get what you want from the development team and from the client, for that matter, is to assume nothing. Don't assume they will know what you want; you will need to explain every single detail and question every single function with the client.

What developers want from you

We talk about scoping a bit later on and I go on and on about how it is important. But from a developer's point of view this is what they normally expect from the designer:

- Designs supplied ready to start build.
- Clearly marked up visuals using pixels for measurements.
- Clear indication of what is live text and what will be displayed as graphics.
- A site map or architecture.
- A scoping document detailing how the functionality works and where the data goes.
- What browser support you would like.
- A sensible schedule, with agreed milestones for testing, bug fixing and development.

There is more about this sort of thing at the end of the book in the section called 10 things...

What you should expect from developers

- Reasonable timescales for build.
- They should test each piece of functionality and check it meets your requirements in the scoping document.
- Work uploaded to a test server and a clear system for feeding back bugs.
- Advance warning of any potential overruns that might occur on development time.
- Code that has been validated and cross platform tested (you will need to ask for this when they estimate).

THE PRINCIPLES OF LAYOUT

Screen sizes and resolution

In the old days it was dead simple, people had small screens, slow connection and no life. They would dial up to the internet on their modem and wait for that familiar sound "shhhh, pu-ching, pu-ching, nar, boing-boing*". In those days, the 'www' stood for the 'world wide wait'. Now people have access to fast connections, giant flat screens and crystal clear mobile devices. This is, of course, all good for the user, but makes life tricky for the designer.

**You never hear this noise any more, I'd like to know how other people would write the connection noise, here's one I found: "Pshhhkkkkkkrrrrk akingkakingkakin gtshchchchchchch chcch*ding*ding* ding."*

Before I even go into the whys and wherefores, all I'll say is: good design is for the best of both worlds because it will never be perfect in either. Design for small screens and great big ones, fast connections and slow ones. Let's look at the scenarios that you might encounter.

The rule used to be: design web pages at a screen size of 800 x 600 pixels, take a bit off for the browser bar (called browser chrome) and a bit off the side for scroll bars and that will do you fine. This led to all manner of weird web pages that hung off the side of the browser or hung around in the top left hand side of the screen waiting for someone to ask it to dance.

The general rule these days is that a web page should be set up to a size of 1024 x 768 pixels (the predictive typing put in 768 pickles – I was very tempted to leave that in). This size tends to work on most computer screens these days, down to the PC laptop and doesn't look too silly on the nice big flat screen.

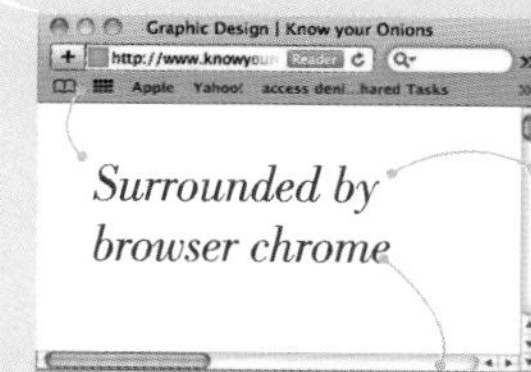

Your design should sit within this width and can be as deep as you like, assuming you don't mind people scrolling down to the floor.

So, we know we have one thousand and twenty four pixels across the width to play with. 'But what is the size of a pixel?', I hear you cry. Well, like Einstein said, 'it's relative'. Let me explain.

If you're unfortunate enough to have spent a month's wages on a ticket to see your favourite rock band at a stadium near you, but find that your seat is at the back of the arena and your guitar hero is the size of a pip, then you will need to look at the screens if you want to see anything at all. The screens they use have a huge 'pixel size'. It does not matter, because you are far enough away that the size of the individual pixel appears to you to be small, but if you were to get up close to one of those screens, each pixel is the size of a plate.

In contrast, your brand new tablet will squeeze as many pixels as it can into the smallest space, making the resolution very high so that when you are watching Gérard Depardieu, you can actually see his nose hairs.

few people will get this 'joke' as it is extremely lame.

So you see, one pixel can be a foot long (Italian herb, please*) or a fraction of a millimetre.

I've seen print designers whack out a PSD (Photoshop) at 350 PPI and when the graphics export they are massive! Resolution is a complex and fickle beast, in this instance – size matters.

In reverse, if you are a print designer, you will be used to clients forever saying things like, "can't you get our logo from the internet?" of course you know if you do use a logo off the internet, when it prints out it will be all pixelated, because the resolution is too low, the pixels will show and your final printed item will not have nice crisp edges.

AS A GENERAL RULE

1024 x 768 pixels @ 72 ppi is an ideal page resolution for most laptop and desk top screens, remember this is not the overall screen resolution of the device, just a guide to the viewable area of a web page.

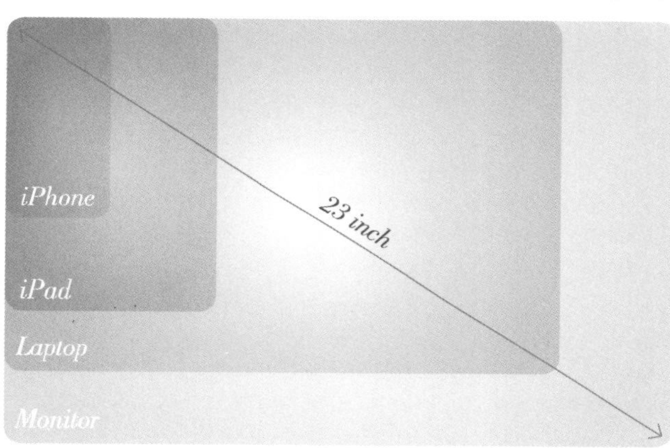

Monitor resolutions:

23 inch monitor:
1600 × 1024 ppi

Laptop:
1024 x 760, 72 ppi

iPad:
1024 × 768, 72 ppi

iPad retina:
2048 × 1536, 72 ppi

iPhone 5 retina:
1136 x 640, 326 ppi

These are just a few examples. There is a vast array of different resolutions and screen sizes. If in doubt, check the specification before you set up the job.

Note: screens are measured in inches, diagonally.

I hinted at the beginning of this section that even though this is a precise science, it is subject to unforeseen influences. I've seen browsers with so many extra bits on them, Google and Yahoo search bars and this and that, the depth of the top of the browser was massive. It must be like viewing the internet through a letter box. Your users will have their browsers set up the way they like them and you cannot control that.

Personally, I like the thinnest browser bar in the world, if I had my way, my browsers would be the width of a cigarette paper.

So, keep in mind that when you are setting up your documents, aligning graphics and what-not, it may look uptown top ranking on your machine, but on Sheila's in accounts screen it may not. Sheila might be the very person who might buy from the very site you are designing; you never know what she gets up to when she leaves work.

***Holy sheep:** that's deep! This is a real user's browser bar.*

This is a really important point and I shouldn't be making light of it by disclosing Sheila's personal shopping habits.

Open up the Google home page on your desk top and phone, search and see how well it renders and oh so slightly different. It responds to the device viewing it – it is responsive.

W3C are a group of noble people who are trying jolly hard to bring some consistent standards to the internet, take a look at: www.w3.org.

It's all too easy to get wrapped up in what you see on your screen and pay no mind to what it will look like elsewhere. If you work in a big enough studio, you will probably have both Macs and PCs. Open a web page in a PC browser, like Explorer, and the same web page on a Mac, in say Safari. Choose a website that isn't one of the big ones, like the BBC or Google, choose a medium-sized company. I suggest this because the big boys spend lots and lots of money trying to sort all these little differences out.

I'm assuming that, as you are reading this book, you don't have access to a massive team of developers and an endless budget like those big website boys and girls have. That is why you need to look at medium to small websites on different browsers and platforms to see what I mean. Most of us have to work with what we have got and get things the best we can, in the realms of reality.

What you will see when viewing the same website on different platforms is varying degrees of change, the website renders differently. There are so many variables, just think about it for a second. Each machine will have an operating system, say OS 10 and then a version, like .2, and perhaps a sub-version: 10.2.1 and that applies to browsers as well. And, of course, each user might not only use a different browser version, but they could be using Firefox, or Chrome. And then there are user preferences, they may have long hair or only ever wear blue shoes and black stockings. The list goes on and on. The variations are huge and as yet, try as the World Wide Web might, there is no consistent standard. Yet.

So, back to the matter in hand. Allow enough tolerances in your design, particularly left and right hand margins to allow for a little variation in display – that way, it will look OK to the majority of people.

Below the fold

A lot of terminology used today has some interesting origins, a bit like the term SPAM (which came from the Monty Python sketch where every dish contained SPAM). 'Below the fold' is an old advertising term. When selling advertising it was cheaper to buy space on the bottom half of the front page of a newspaper. You see, most newspapers you buy at the newsstand are folded in half; the cheaper space was 'below the fold'.

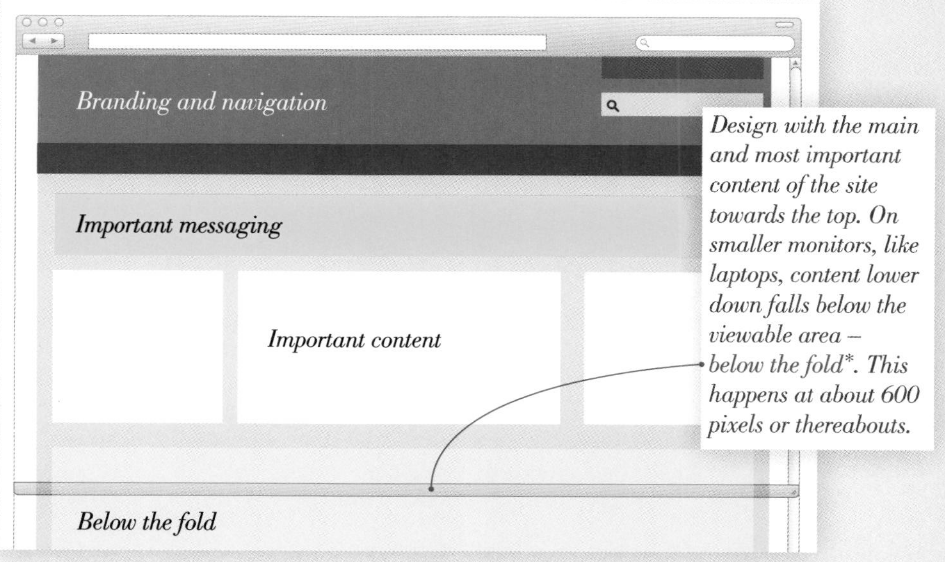

Design with the main and most important content of the site towards the top. On smaller monitors, like laptops, content lower down falls below the viewable area – below the fold. This happens at about 600 pixels or thereabouts.*

When the term is used in our case, web design, it refers to what you can see when the page loads in the browser, without having to scroll down. This is the prime real estate on web pages; anything above the fold is instantly viewable. That colleague (consider giving the colleague a name) I mentioned (Sheila) that has stacks of stuff on their top browser bar will be able to see less, the fold will be higher in effect.

**Roughly: this isn't an exact thing, the fold varies from user to user, but roughly speaking.*

The anatomy of a web page

Every web page on every site is different. And so it should be. But there are common elements and structures that make up a typical page. The illustration to the right only shows a few examples of some content types, with a view to helping you understand the terminology and general placement of these elements on a very typical page structure.

Like I say, these elements move around, change shape and are not always appropriate. Generally, websites have some or all of these elements. Shown here they all align perfectly with matching gutters held together on the 960 grid.

See page 75 for all you need to know about 960 grids.

The page includes:
H1: Headline
The main headline for the page.

H2: Second headline
This style can also be used for a standfirst.

Body text
The main text style and I have chosen an underline to show a link and a small inset image.

Call to action
A highlighted call to action, which could of course be anything from 'Buy me' to 'Donate' or a link to a more in-depth article.

An advert or sign up panel
Usually a fairly high profile piece of content, but may fall below the fold.

Logo and masthead
This is where the main site branding sits.

Horizontal navigation
The top level navigation, perhaps with dropdowns for sub-sections.

Left hand navigation
Can be used as the sole navigation or in combination with the horizontal navigation.

Image
The main image on the page, often a carousel.

Login and Search bar

Footer
This tends to hold repeated 'live text links' from the main navigation set, the T&Cs and site map and credits. That sort of thing.

Promo panels
These little panels take centre stage, after the main content has been read, usually below the fold.

Right hand or associated content panels
These panels could be adverts, or highlighted products that relate to main page content.

The illustration below shows the heat zones. Even without using eye-tracking technology, it makes sense that a user's eyes will linger in the areas shown.

Hot spots and zones

Somebody, I'm not sure who, must have been someone with time on their hands and perhaps eats a lot of takeaway pizza, ran some experiments that tracked web user's eyes whilst searching the internet. I can only speculate what the results looked like, bearing in mind a that large proportion of internet traffic is of the 'adult' nature. Anyway, the research showed that users' eyes tend to linger on blondes in bikinis and shiny six-packs, sorry wrong book, on certain areas of the screen. This creates 'hot zones' that are handy to know about, if you want to highlight something or place importance on an item navigation, for instance.

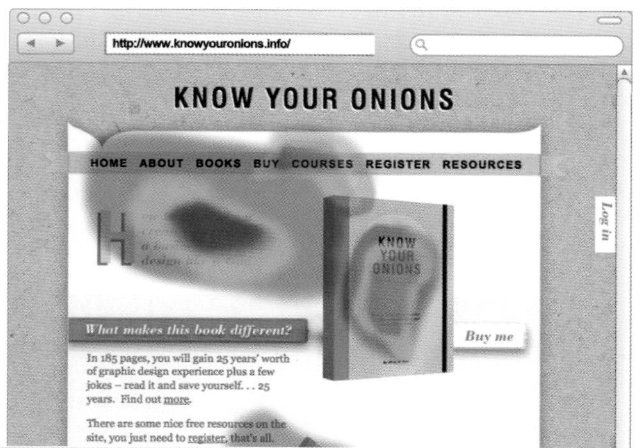

The shapes indicate the length of time viewing a certain area. Red being the longest.

My advice to you is not to share this sort of information with clients as they will try to get you to put everything in these areas, 'a little knowledge is a bad thing' and all that. I had one client, an ex-banker whom I am not saying fitted any ex-banker type of stereotype but did, who started a gold buying website, which he thought was going to be a 'cash goldmine'. He used to go on and on about research and findings and this and that. He essentially read articles online, which of course must be true, and so directed 'my' design so much he ended up with a poor interface. He then blamed the fact that the users kept bouncing when they visited the website and didn't pay his bill. God only knows what he would have tried to make me do if he had proper user testing data instead of his conspiracy theories. Good luck to him, I can't tell you what his site is, of course.

Grids

Just like print design, grids are the hidden structure that hold the content together. Most designs have a grid unless they don't – if you see what I mean. In web design, they serve the same purpose as they do in print design, but they also have the potential to cock things up. But before I get 'grid negative', let's get 'grid positive'.

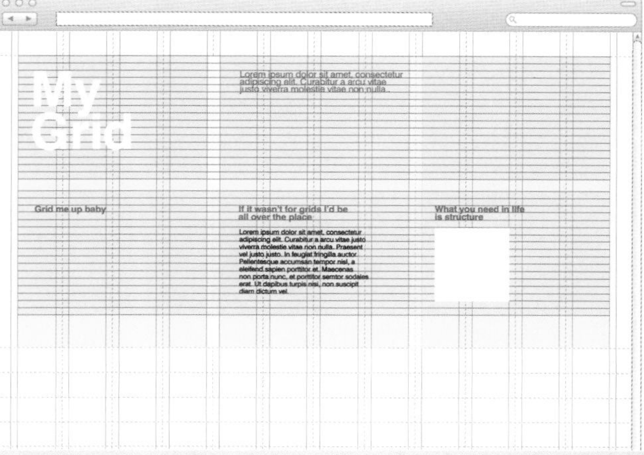

Even if you are using a template grid as a starting point, you will need to edit and add to your grids to make sure your design 'hangs together'. Use guides to ensure all items align. Make sure you have 'snap to guides' switched on and even then, make sure you get things placed exactly. If you don't, when the developer slices up your PSDs, he probably won't notice that something is slightly out, and you will notice when he's built it. It can be a right pain in the Rupert for him if he has to go back and reposition items for you. Try to be pixel perfect.

You can ask the developer to put character limits on the editable text but they always end up really messy and sentences end up fini...

Vertical guides mean everything will align nicely, but horizontal guides on your grid can cause problems later on. It is a problem we come across time and time again. Let's say you split your page up into three or four columns with an 'article' starting at each column.

You will design it so that it looks great in Photoshop and all the paragraphs are roughly the same depth. But when the real content goes in, life will not be like that. So let that dream go. Don't listen to the client or content editor when they say,

"No problem, we can write the articles to fit", because they won't. They never ever do.

It's easier to illustrate with a picture. Below, you can see a very nice and organised grid with all the content behaving well and not getting unruly or having ideas of its own.

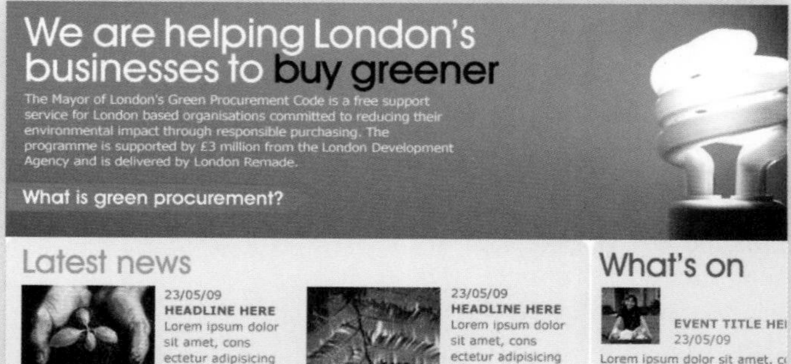

The second illustration is the same, post revolution, where the political junta has done away with the very foundation and cement of content control and allowed them to run wild.

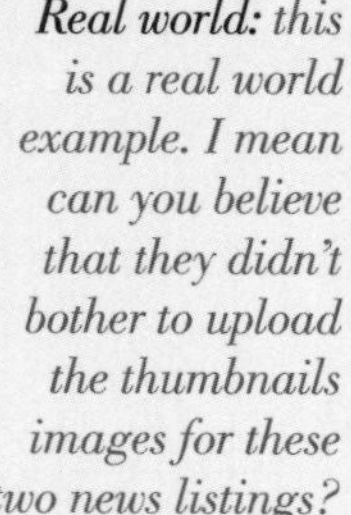

Real world: this is a real world example. I mean can you believe that they didn't bother to upload the thumbnails images for these two news listings?

This is what happens in the real world.

960 grids

A time ago, I forget when, the web design industry adopted the 960 grid system. The grids come in 12, 16 and 24 columns across a 1024 pixel width and provide the guides for gutters and columns for designers and developers. It is designed so that the site elements are all contained in this width. The nice thing about the system is not only does it help the designer align elements, but it also provides the developer with the basic code to help them position these items correctly. They are a great starting point and make our lives easier. The templates themselves come in a stack of formats so that you can use them in an array of applications. They are easy to find online, but, because I'm nice, you can download them here: www.knowyouronions.info. There isn't a lot to say about them other than that really. It is important to consider when you are working within the grids to understand what is a gutter guide and how to divide up the grid to give you equal columns. You'll see what I mean, when you take a look at the typical page structures that follow: these are designed on a 960 grid.

A great big thank you to Nathan Smith: 960.gs

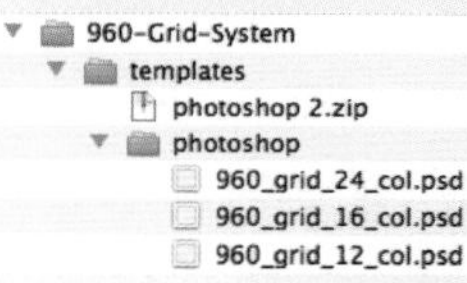

Typical page structures

In our design world we would all like everything we do to be 100 per cent unique and never been seen before. But we all know life isn't like that, wheels are round, pens are thin and sushi portions are small. There are some very handy starting points that can be customised to help web designers on their way. That is all they are, starting points – if you begin to use them for everything, then everything will begin to look the same.

Obviously, the page structures will be defined by the content. Not every website will want a highly prominent sign up form, or a news panel or whatever. But in my experience, what I offer in the next few pages will start you off good and proper.

Potentially, there are a lot of variables to contend with. Designing any website, you will see as you progress that you can mix up alignments, structure and content to give you endless solutions. And then I start talking about Japanese food, which requires a leap of faith.

Floating panel

This is one of my favourites; it can be applied to so many situations and generally looks good on most screen sizes. It allows you to have bright or subtle backgrounds and the content feels like it is all retained on a clearly defined page. Floating panels are really only good for small sites with a low level of content.

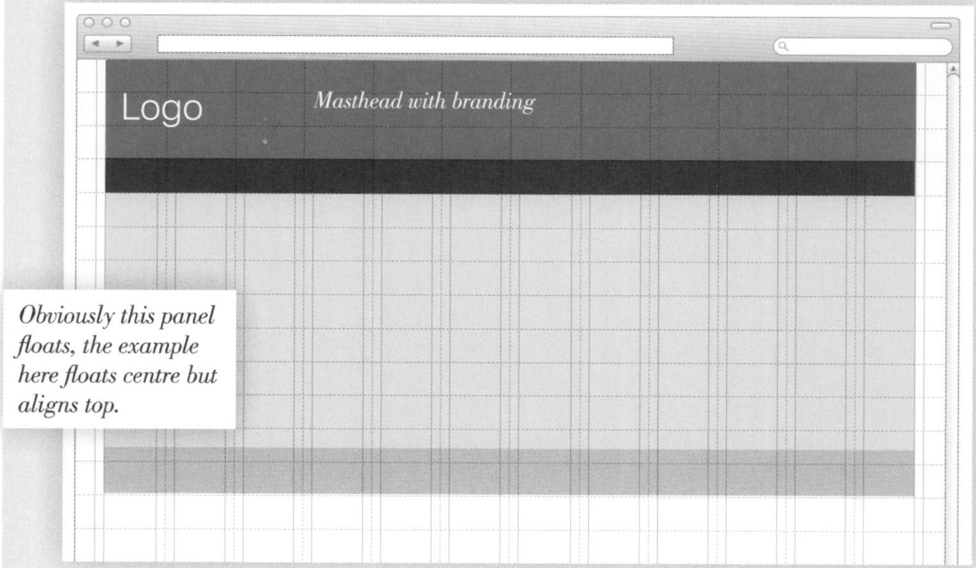

Obviously this panel floats, the example here floats centre but aligns top.

100 per cent width sites are not very popular these days because, I suspect, computer monitor sizes vary so much. Essentially, the content width expands and contracts to suit the browser window size. This means that content moves about as you resize your browser. You'd think this might be

a good idea, because this technique is designed to adjust for different monitor sizes – that's the point. Except that it generally looks awful. Unless... isn't there always an exception (that apparently proves the rule)? Unless the design is responsive.

Responsive Design sorts this problem out and is the new darling of web design, for the moment. I shall introduce you to this new darling later on, when I know you a bit more.

100 per cent width can come in handy with things like top bars and horizontal bars so that they always 'bleed' off the edge of the browser. You can combine that with a fixed width content area, perhaps centred, and the site stands up to a wide variety of situations.

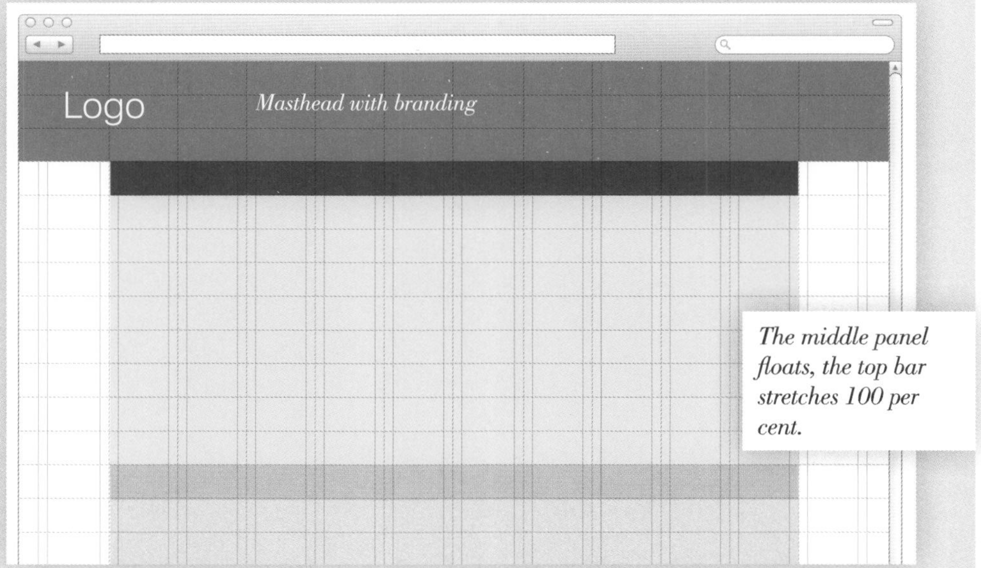

The middle panel floats, the top bar stretches 100 per cent.

Letterbox

Letterbox designs are very handy for websites where images are more important than lots of text. We use them for things like restaurants and micro-sites. The 'letterbox' area does not necessarily have to bleed, in fact, when you allow for a graphic to fit in a 1024 pixel width and then view it on a 32-inch flat screen, a 100 per cent width can look very odd with the content floating all alone in the middle.

Letterbox designs do make sub-pages and sub-navigation integration a tad difficult. The central panel dominates the home page, usually, and when it disappears or shortens its depth on sub-pages, the other elements in the design seem

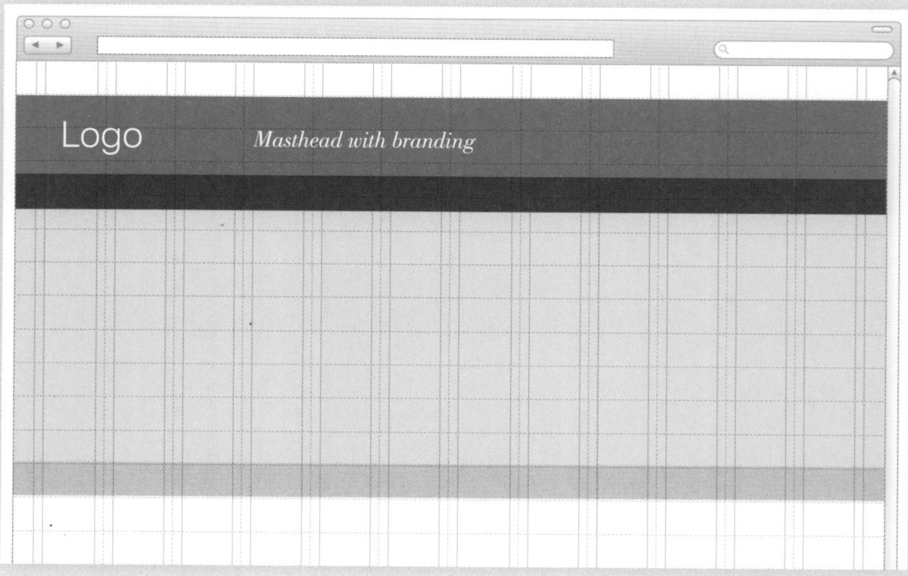

to sort of sit about looking dejected. So, if you do opt for a letterbox design, think hard about how you will integrate the sub-pages and sub-navigation.

Horse shoe

Websites with a lot of content and a lot of what we call 'associated content' – which is content that sits alongside the main content and usually directs the user to content that might be similar or of interest to them – need a structure that is flexible and can deal with volume.

This structure allows for horizontal navigation, a left hand navigation and a right hand column for, as I say, associated content, or sign up panels or all manner of bits and bobs.

There are, of course, oodles of different structures you can work with, but I shall linger no longer, this book has a wider remit. Onwards.

'I shall linger no longer' would make a great song title.

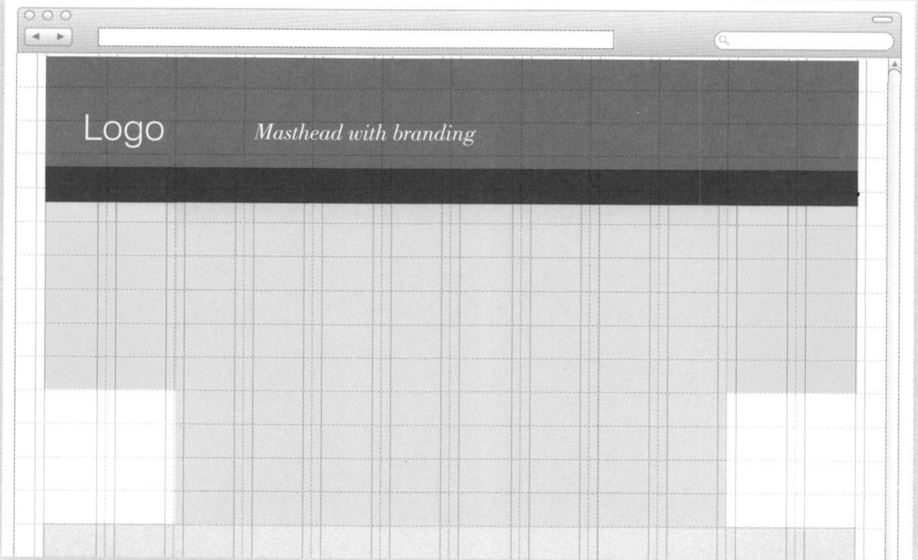

Page alignment

When you have got your head around page structures, you will need to give a moment's thought to how the page is aligned. We are not talking about whether the text is range left or centred – we are talking about the whole page or at least the whole content area.

Centred text can be the Devil in terms of readability, in both web and print design. Be cautious when clients request 'balanced and centred text' as the Devil cares only for himself and not the readership.

"The Devil may have the best tunes" as they say, but "God is in the details". Attributed to Ludwig Mies van der Rohe, a chap well worth looking up.

Different structures lend themselves to different alignments. For instance floating panels lend themselves to being centred, fixed width often work with aligning top and left as well as centred. Nothing works aligning right or aligning bottom.

Parallax

With new technology come new trends and the darlings (as I write) are responsive websites and parallax scrolling. I think it's fair to argue that responsive is born out of necessity whereas parallax is just cool.

A website built using parallax scrolling is basically one great big long page: when you click on a link in the navigation (horizontal most of the time) the page scrolls down automatically to that section. It's nice to watch as the content scoots past, slipping under the navigation until you come to rest on the section you are interested in. As I say, the navigation stays where it is.

With some fancy coding, background elements can follow you down the page, perhaps arriving a little later than the main content and 'easing' in. Parallax websites are no good for websites with lots of content or stacks of pages, they serve brochure-ware sites where style rules the day.

I've seen some hopelessly unusable parallax sites that don't even have navigation, just a tiny arrow pointing down. How hard can you make it for people? Why make it hard at all?

The space

Partners

About

The team

Events

FAQ

Contact

Home
This is the viewable area for most screens. The rest of the page loads underneath.

When a user clicks a button on the main navigation (shown below), the whole page scrolls up, and under the navigation bar (so it is always there) to the relevant section. If for instance the user clicked 'Contact' the the whole page would whizz past their very eyes.

The problems with parallax

- Can be slow to load.
- Content has to be short.
- Hard to scale up and add new sections.
- Difficult to implement sub-navigation/pages.
- Can bamboozle the user.
- No good for SEO.

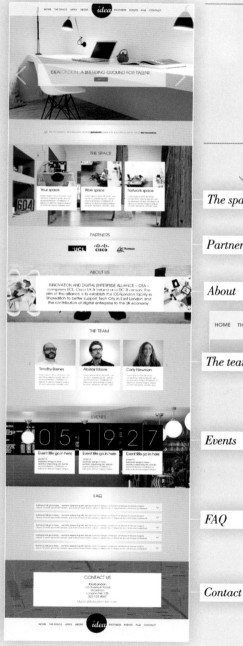

Responsive

A responsive design (or a Responsive Web Design (RWD)) reacts to certain situations instead of ignoring the situation and hoping it will go away. Like a good General, a responsive design rises to the challenge of a changing environment and adapts. Users with different devices, screen sizes and environments are tackled head on. The content and the design is repurposed to suit the device the users are viewing it on. That way, the content is delivered in the optimum way for the device, to minimise scrolling and resizing content to give the best user experience.

I have to tackle this subject from a designer's point of view. And, if I am honest, it won't be enough to make you an expert responsive designer.

Above: *the content responds to the device display and important items are given priority over lesser items.*

A responsive web design uses a fluid grid that moves and alters the content to fit the user's device. You can spot a website that has been designed in a responsive way by making your browser window smaller and if the content changes, images resize, navigation moves, then boy, oh boy, it has responded. Responsive sites use media queries to establish what device you are using and how best to repurpose the content to give the best user experience. Depending on the width of the viewing device, content is resized or stacked on top of each other, based on a priority. Things like the clickable area of a link, the entire removal of some elements, and the way the typography is presented can change with responsive design.

I did say I would touch on this – it is another book in itself.

The Bento box

You know when you go for a Japanese meal you sometimes get your food in a little box that is divided into little compartments? They are called Bento boxes. What on Earth have Bento boxes got to do with web design? Just hang on a minute while I eat my sushi.

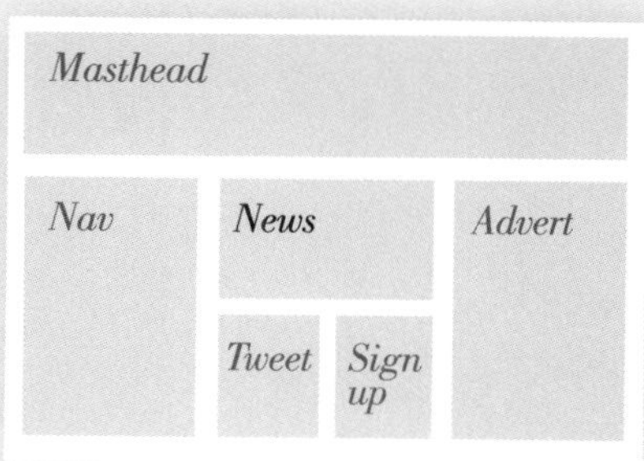

When you are designing websites that have a number of different elements of functionality or content types, your page is essentially broken down into different compartments. And like a Bento box, you can choose what type of content you want to go into any compartment. These compartments can move and even change shape, but they remain compartments.

The content types fit into the containers which in turn sit on a grid. Below, the same content types have changed shape. For instance, on one web page a 'News' panel might be across two coloumns, on another it might only be across one.

This is a really good principle to get your head around, it is essential when you are designing websites that will be built using content management systems (CMS).

If your website is going to have an integrated Twitter panel, a news headline panel and a sign up panel, each one of these essentially gets put in a box (sometimes called a container), so it makes sense that these containers could move about and change shape.

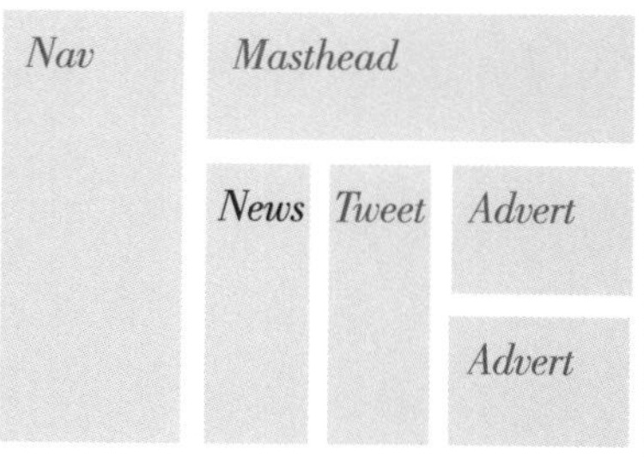

To the right I have tried to show you two scenarios of how a web page, with the same content types can be displayed differently. You will need to remember that if any of your designs are graphic based, you will need to supply graphics for all scenarios, your graphics can't change shape, and you will need a new graphic for each sizing. After all, graphics are 'fixed' items; you have to make a new one, for each width or depth.

It will make a lot more sense when you start designing and working with a CMS.

A real Bento box

THE PRINCIPLES OF COLOUR

Colour, of course, plays a huge part in the life and times of a designer. There are lots of theories about colour out there – people say lilac makes you fall in love with cats and orange can be used to simulate a sun tan. I'll not go into that here. I will go into some tricks when using colour to get easily achievable effects, as well as helping you to understand the different 'spaces' colours work in. It is a massive subject. You'd be very surprised the number of designers in full-time employment who don't know the basics of colour and the 'types' of colour. So, don't be in the dark, see the light and read on!

C M Y K

Your printer probably has four cartridges, cyan, magenta, yellow and black, which are all designed to run out at different times, but seriously, this mode of colour is not the same mode as a screen and that is why it will never look the same.

Colours for screen and print

First things first, no matter how expensive your kit is, what you see on screen will not be what you see on the printed sheet. It is also unlikely that it will look the same on other people's monitors either. Macintosh and PC monitors can vary hugely, then there are lighting conditions, the monitor settings and whether the user is wearing rose-tinted glasses or not.

Web designers have to aim for the best possible compromise, print designers will aim for perfection and never really achieve it.

There is a thing called gamut, it means the 'space' or the range of colours that can be seen in a certain gamut. Our eyes have a very wide gamut and can see a massive range of colours. However, any output device, a printer or a screen for example, has a limited gamut; they cannot display the full range of colours the eye can see, just yet.

R G B

As far as the web designer is concerned, there are two main modes, spaces or whatever you want to call them that you need to be aware of – RGB and Hexadecimal. There is also HSB, hue, saturation and brightness, I'll enlighten you shortly.

B

#000000

W

#FFFFFF

#FF0000

***Hex:** three hexadecimal colour codes*

Colour modes and colour pickers

It is always best to select colours using the correct colour picker (or palette) and that fit in the right gamut for the output device, for us that will be a screen. RGB will be the mode you should set your web design documents up in, it's ridiculous to work in a mode like CMYK, which is a mode for print. The file size will be massive, you will have fewer colours to choose from and the colours will appear 'flatter' on screen. So use RGB.

RGB will enable you to use all the nice things you will want to use, like gradients and eye popping combinations. Monitors use RGB lights to create full colour images and jolly good they are too.

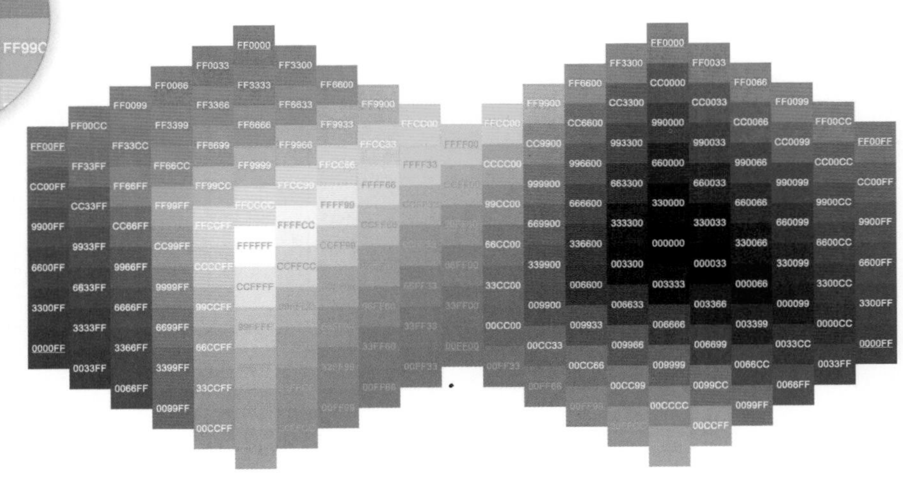

Hexadecimal is a colour system that browsers use to define flat colours or solid colours (I'm simplifying here before you write in saying "Dear Drew, with reference to your limited understanding of Hexadecimal colours..."). Hex colours start with a hash (#), not a hallucinogenic substance, and are followed by a 6 number/letter combination. These numbers alter the colour reference and of course the display. You can select your colours in lots of different ways, using colour pickers, sliders, droppers and other ways that sound like slang for criminals.

These two colour pickers are essentially the same, except the values in the top one are shown in RGB, the bottom in Hexadecimal.

To keep things consistent, build a palette for your website using real and precise values in Hexadecimal, then everything will match.

I'm a piece of Verdana and I could be a link, but then again, so could I... confusing eh?

Coloured type within text usually indicates the piece of type is a link, as does an underline, choose one and be consistent.

Putting a colour palette together

Again, this could be a book in itself, but I don't have time for all of that. So, a good trick when working with a palette is to select a colour, and when you want a nice, darker colour to compliment it, just add 10 per cent of black – this nearly always works. Also, when putting together a large range of colours in your palette, try and select colours of a similar tone. A bright green and a dusty blue do not tend to make good bedfellows.

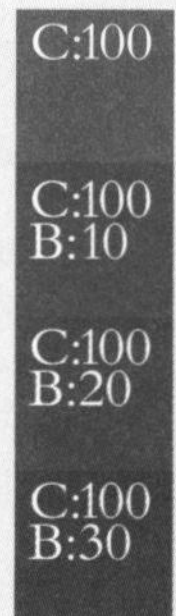

10 per cent of black added to cyan to create a harmonious palette: taking it one step further, just reduce the percentage of the cyan and the black. This is the palette used in this book.

Adobe (who spell about as well as I do) have a web app called 'Kuler' which is a great tool for putting together colour palettes or viewing colour themes that other users have created. It just helps you look at things from a slightly different perspective every now and then.

The use of colour is a bit like the use of typography; pick a key colour and keep it simple, less is more. Oh, and don't colour up too much type – it is harder to read and looks naff.

Pinhole effect: I multiplied my vignette over the image and stretched it to fit. It looks good and also fixed that horrible white corner bottom right.

Images and illustrations

By images, I usually mean photographs. Like any design, photographs and illustrations help to enhance your message and make your design visually appealing. I've already told you not to knick stuff, so setting that aside, I'll run through some do's and don'ts to help you select and integrate your imagery to achieve the best effects.

Instagram does a brilliant job of making even the worst photograph look good. It does this by using filters, as you probably know. If you are using images that are not from Instagram, which will be most of the time, you can recreate these effects in Photoshop. The most useful technique (good for print design as well) is to create a 'pinhole camera' effect. Do this by overlaying a black and white spherical graduation over the top of your image, scale to fit the entire image and use 'overlay' on the layers palette. Adjust the opacity, subtle is usually best, so use a low opacity. Nice.

When selecting images, try to choose ones that have a similar style. For instance, close up and with a short depth of field, as they will look best when sitting together. If the images on your site need a retro feel, desaturate them. Mixing images that are photographs with 'quirky' graphics very rarely works and looks amateurish. Using clip art (anagram: crap lit) should be avoided at all costs and reserved for the type of people who compose their emails in Comic Sans.

Don't just plonk them on the page using the same crop as they were provided in. Take time to look at the image and crop it to gain the best results. This kind of consideration is woefully neglected a lot of the time and the difference that a well-cropped image makes is enormous.

As a rule of thumb, an image that is composed in 'middle distance' tends to be a bit dull. We don't want dull, do we? So, either go long distance or right in close to get the best and most engaging composition.

Rule of thirds

Do you know about the rule of thirds? You should. To my loyal readership who kindly bought my other book, you will notice I have been a lazy sod and lifted this section, but to the trained eye, you may also notice – and in my defence – that I have added a few extra titbits.

The rule of thirds is very well known. Photographers are always told to think in thirds, which must be tough when ordering in restaurants. The principles still apply to layout and can be applied to graphic design in lots of different scenarios. When designing magazine spreads for instance, applying the rule can give you a nice starting point for your layout.

The rule states: divide the area your 'image' will occupy. When positioning the main focus of your image, align the item where the first or last third in the grid intersects. Easier to show than explain. Have a look right.

Focal point: place the main focus of your image at the intersection as opposed to the middle of the crop.

Don't just plonk the focus of attention in the middle of the crop, use the rule of thirds, allow the item to breathe with a reasonable amount of space around it, as this helps to create more impact than making it as big as you can.

Icons

Clients think that if you use icons, users will understand what they mean and it will give them a fast and graphically engaging way for them (the users) to navigate the site. They are wrong.

I was called into a government department in the UK to help design a user interface for a massive system. This was a closed, intranet site that enabled users to search current planning applications, pending planning applications and past applications. What this bit of kit did was enable a select set of users to view all the building and planning applications across London and sort, export, view or do anything they wanted, via this interface. I met the guy who built it. It took him years. I got called in because his boss said, "It works and the whole thing does what it should, but nobody can use it. Design some icons to make it easier". So I sat with the guy who built it and he explained what it did. It was amazing.

He showed me the home interface, with his icons, the ones I had been called into redesign. And I said, as I covered up the rest of the screen, what does this icon mean? (Compass). What does this icon mean? (A pair of scissors) and what does this mean? (A folder.) Not one person in the meeting could answer, not even the guy who built it.

The simple reason is that icons only work when they are recognised, and there are very few out there. Below is a set of icons. What do they mean in the context of a website that enables users to view planning permissions across London?

Any idea what any of these mean? Imagine trying to use these to navigate the site!

They mean nothing. And the reason they mean nothing is because people don't instantly understand them. This happens with brands. Everybody wants the same recognition as the Nike swoosh. But understand this, the only reason the Nike swoosh is recognised is because they have a million pound (dollar/corona/denarius etc.) budget so they can slap their logo on everything you see and do it all over the globe.

Designing HTML emails

Designing HTML emails is similar to designing web pages in some ways, but with more restrictions. There are a lot of templates out there and some of them are very, very good. If you are using a service to broadcast (mass mail) your emails, then the broadcast companies usually have templates that are ready to edit and that is fine for a quick fix. To be honest, your client could customise the templates themselves and they would be OK, but they wouldn't be great, because they are templates. This book isn't about templates.

Before we get into the nitty gritty of design, let's establish some principles.

I am not an expert on monks or what they get up to on the internet, but I do know that monks are experts at restraint.

What they need to do

HTML emails are like adverts or newsletters popping into your inbox. We all get SPAM in our mailboxes from the African prince who wants to transfer his inheritance into your bank account, to emails offering you performance-enhancing drugs. We also get added to mailing lists for things we may or may not want. And so, we get mailed rubbish most of the time. The best HTML emails are the ones you want to read: they have content tailored to you, they are of specific interest to you. So we'll leave the dodgy practitioners to themselves and we will continue to delete them.

The aim of an e-vite, e-newsletter or e-com or whatever you want to call it is to interest your reader enough to get them wanting more. This usually means them clicking through to the website. This may seem obvious, but the point here is to keep to the brief. I've seen emails that have so much content in them, they would be a website on their own.

The content should be a synopsis of an article or a clear offer that can be read in seconds and be so enticing it would require monk-like restraint not to click through and read more.

I don't purport to be the world's greatest expert on e-newsletter design, but I do know a thing or two and I'll do my best to impart my knowledge. Overleaf is a diagram of 'the anatomy of an HTML newsletter' marked up with what does what and a bit about why this one is good. This is only a 'typical style', you can design them any way you like, but remember, an e-newsletter is a taster, it is a middle ground between an advert and an article on a web page.

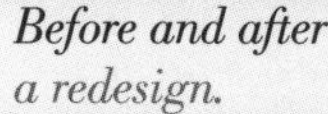

Before and after a redesign.

The anatomy of an HTML newsletter

The structure below is of course, only an example, you can see it in action overleaf. This basic structure can be seen applied to the other examples later on.

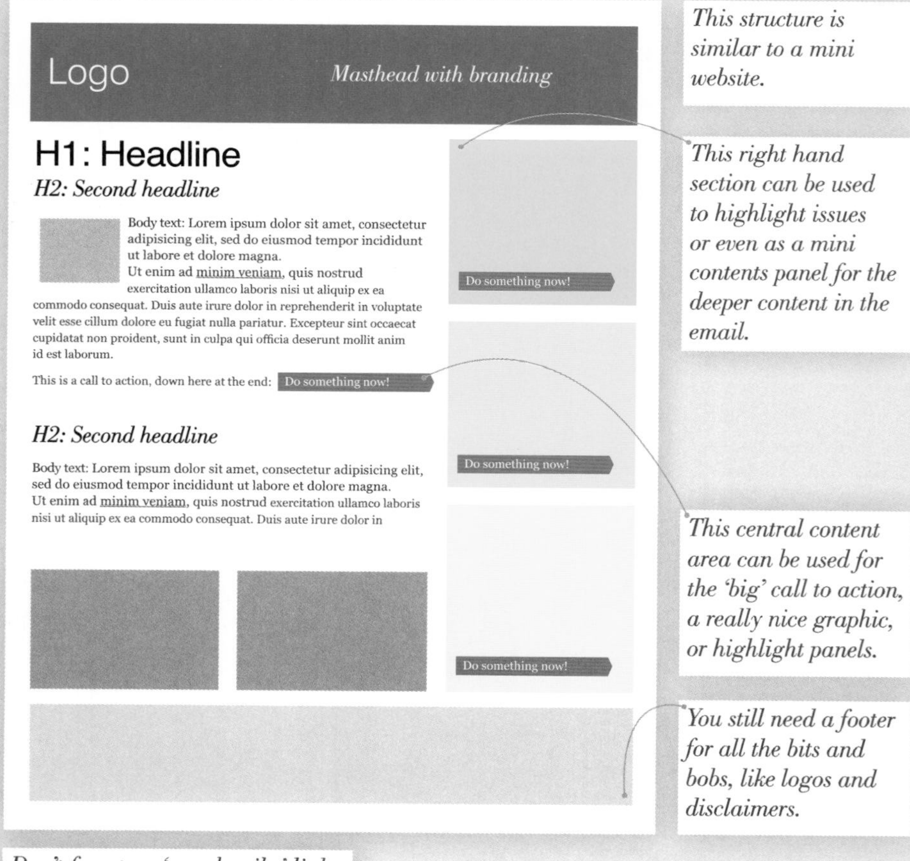

This structure is similar to a mini website.

This right hand section can be used to highlight issues or even as a mini contents panel for the deeper content in the email.

This central content area can be used for the 'big' call to action, a really nice graphic, or highlight panels.

You still need a footer for all the bits and bobs, like logos and disclaimers.

Don't forget an 'unsubscribe' link, people get jolly annoyed if they can't find a way of removing themselves from a list.

Typical HTML email styles

There is no set style to anything, let's face it. If you want to design a pair of trousers with three legs – why not? And why not, indeed. I've only met two people with three legs and I'm comfortably sure that three legged trousers are in short supply, but for the rest of us two legged homo sapiens, the two legged variety will do. So in a round about way, what I am saying is, if you are designing an HTML email, e-shot, e-newsletter or even an e-blast (which sounds like a terrible bathroom situation), designing a newsletter that will be delivered via email, in the two legged variety, they come in a few standard types. So, this is what I think makes up the best emails, and whether they work, or not.

Below: this HTML email has a lot of content, but the way it has been broken up into chunks makes it engaging.

Delivering the news

There are organisations out there that actually need to deliver news. This is a proper newsletter. We are talking about articles of interest and an audience who wants to read more. This is how the whole e-newsletter started and the best examples follow a magazine cover and contents page. The newsletter needs to do what these two things do in a print form, bang in the middle of an inbox. These are:

- Wow, what a great issue, different from the last, I must read on.
- OK, here is the synopsis of the newsletter so you know what you are getting.
- Here is a taster of the article, it is so interesting, how can I not click through and read more?
- Here is the call to action, I love this, where can I 'buy one' or whatever your call to action is.

This is how to do it.

Buy me, I'm on offer

My life, how many offers come into your inbox a day? Oodles. And what do you buy? Probably not a lot – when you do it is more likely than not because the offers are tailored to you or because they know what you want or may want to buy. In order to serve the right offers and content (doesn't always need to be offers), the company sending the e-shot needs to know a bit about you. There is probably a book out there called Know Your Onions: Data, but that is definitely not the book for me, although I think my wife would love it.

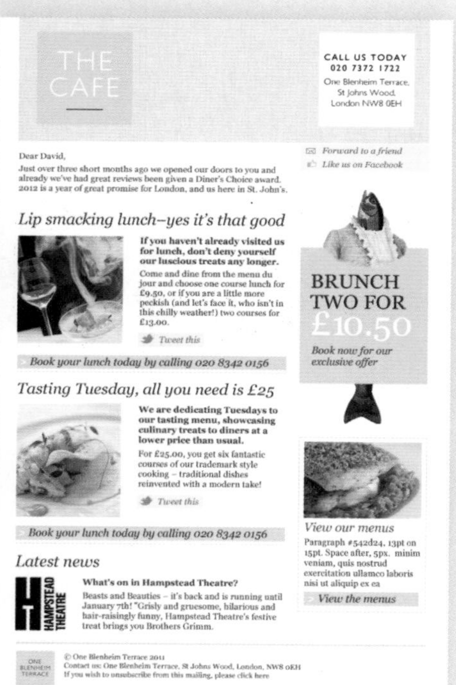

On offer: this newsletter goes out to regular subscribers, but clearly features an offer to be had.

My mission, assuming you choose to accept it, is to help you design great HTML emails for companies that know their consumers and clients and highlight the right offers and services to make them happy. The first aim here is to avoid every precious member of your list not to unsubscribe. The least you can hope for is to keep them on the list, that way if they are not interested this time, they might be the next.

Marketing bods will try to make every e-com (notice the myriad phrases to name what is essentially an email with pictures) do and say everything. For some markets this works OK. For instance, in the restaurant industry a subscriber may want to know about an offer, what's new on the menu or wine list and the odd snippet of news or culinary advice. But start spreading it thin with a market that has more direct and unique requirements, say S&M (look it up) who may not be interested in where the rubber is manufactured, you must stick to your message and give the readership what they want.

The structure shown left will work-ish, for a wine expert, an IT obsessive and anybody who may have particular tastes in leather or rubber.

How cool am I?

I bought an iPod speaker from a French company just because I loved the email. Seriously. I've read reviews on all manner of speakers, but this just got me, so I bought it. Didn't look at a review, never heard the thing working. But boy, oh boy did the e-blast (another name, collect the set) light my fire. These designs tend to be graphic heavy, which has its issues, but done well, they are the ultimate advert in your inbox.

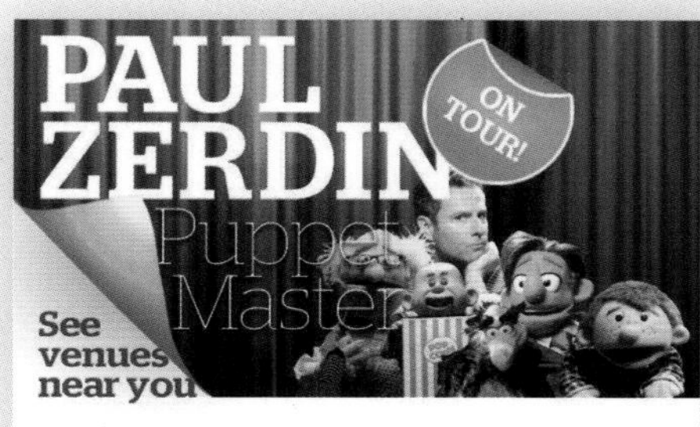

PAUL
ZERDIN
ON TOUR!
Puppet
Master
See venues near you
Paul Zerdin has returned with a great new show.
Catch him this Summer at the following venues all around the UK. The Puppet Master tour boasts brand new jokes and a new member to Pauls fuzzy friends.
Up-coming tour dates
July
27 Hall for Cornwall, Truro BUY NOW
28 Pavilion, Weymouth BUY NOW
August
02 Embassy Theatre, Skegness BUY NOW
03 Britannia Pier Theatre, Gt. Yarmouth BUY NOW
04 Spa Pavilion, Felixstowe BUY NOW
09 Pavilion, Worthing BUY NOW
10 Shanklin Theatre, IOW BUY NOW
24 Floral Pavilion, New Brighton BUY NOW
25 Pavilion Theatre, Rhyl BUY NOW
30 Embassy Theatre, Skegness BUY NOW
31 Britannia Pier Theatre, Gt. Yarmouth BUY NOW
September
01 Princes Theatre, Clacton BUY NOW
Ask Albert!
Ask Albert a question now and he'll answer it live at the show of your choice.
Ask him
ONLINE VIDEOS

But, here is the rub: like print design, each HTML newsletter, blast, com or whatever, must be designed for its purpose. If it is to deliver news, it must look newsworthy (like a newsletter does in print), or look like an advert that evoks a response (like an advert in the press). It is up to yoú to decide, when you get the brief and the text, what kind of e-shot you should design.

Sizes

Variables, variables, variables. How on earth do I get my email to look great for everyone? You won't. But the basic principles are to keep the content narrow, the good stuff at the top and the call to action underneath each item that needs one. For instance, 'Half price pizza on Mondays for everybody (offer), tell us your favourite toppings, the best combos get entered into a draw (competition) – enter now, closing date Friday' – (that is the call to action).

Go back to the examples above, they show you best practice. But in terms of sizes, keep your width around 600-700 pixels wide. This is a good size because a user will see most if not all in the 'preview pane' in their email client (program). Keep the depth as short as you can. An email is a taster, not a web page.

Idea: Top Trumps of e-coms, you could judge the quality of the design by assigning points to: call to action, the offer and relevance of the offer, with extra points for bold design and clarity. Good idea?

While I think this looks nice and I designed it, it's not best practice...

Technical constraints

Email programs cannot display or offer the same functionality that a web page can. Not yet anyway. And one hates to predict the future, but by the time they can render the full web experience, email may not be around in the form you now know it. I suspect lawyers might end up using it after we have all moved on. No matter, as I write, that is the way things are.

...the problem with it is, it has way too many graphics.

Today and not necessarily in the future, HTML emails are built using 'old' technology. They are built like old websites used to be, using tables. These are code structures that comprise of cells, set out in columns and rows. This framework houses the content of your email and jolly awkward it is too. This type of structure can be restricting and prone to breaking. Often you find developers struggling to accommodate designs within this type of build. But then, that's life and until that changes, there is little we can do about it, so know your restrictions before you design and design to meet the technological constraints – that's your job.

There are a host of constraints when designing a HTML email that simply can't be achieved when built. I don't know them all, but here are a few.

Graphics in the background

You cannot put graphics, textures or images in the background of an email. So what that means is, you cannot put a picture behind a piece of live text, you have to make the text part of the image. You can colour the cell, you can make it solely an image, but not both.

Tables: below is a very rough outline of the structure for the top part of the Know Your Onions *HTML email.*

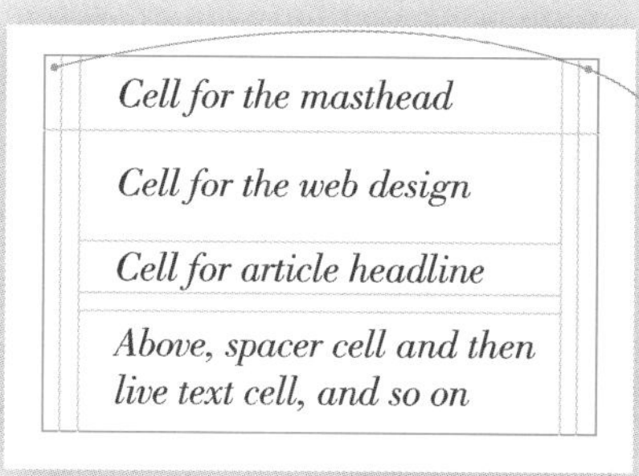

Text falling in different levels

If you design your email to have multiple columns and the content they hold is 'live' i.e. not a graphic, you run the very real risk of the text running to different lengths. You need a very disciplined copywriter to get it right. Only ever seen it done right once. See below right.

Cell for the masthead

Cell for the web design

Cell for article headline

Above, spacer cell and then live text cell, and so on

Column for those little ribbons

Big graphics

This is why my email design was poor, I used loads of graphics. If the recipient has graphics turned off then almost no content will be visible when it lands in the inbox.

Widths

You need to design them with the fact that most recipients will be viewing them in the preview pane of their email client, so 600 pixels and no more.

Limited functionality

Emails are mini web pages, but you cannot integrate functionality into an email like you can a website. All those forms, polls, video, etc. need to be hosted elsewhere and you can link out to them. Embedded video is almost here.

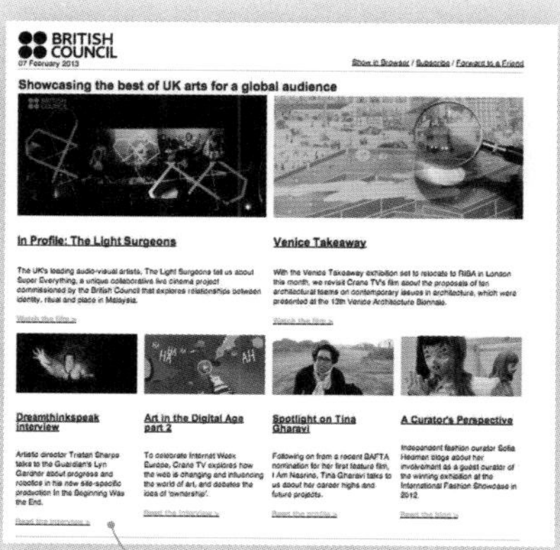

Almost perfect: but not quite, best I've seen in terms of self-control with copy.

Added irritation

This could be a long list, but too much coloured text, horrible backgrounds and really long articles will irritate just about everybody.

THE PRINCIPLES OF NAVIGATION

Where am I? Where have I come from? Where can I go?

This is going to sound obvious, and if you get it right, nobody will even notice: get it wrong and you risk annoying the heck out of your users. Your navigation system should be able to answer the questions above, no matter how big the site is, without the user even having to think.

Navigation is probably the single most important thing to consider when designing your website. The type (style) and structure of your navigation will depend on the level of content your site will have to accommodate. Don't underestimate the task, it needs careful thought before you start your design and with a keen eye to the future. The future is where poorly considered navigation suffers a breakdown.

Let's deal with the questions above, one by one.

Where am I?

Well, at the moment, I'm in Norfolk writing this on the beach. Seriously, a user should always know, when looking at the navigation where they are in the site, no matter how deep they are in the content. If they are on the home page, it's easy: the home button will be highlighted with the hit state and they have probably just arrived at the site so, life couldn't be simpler.

But, don't assume users will automatically arrive on the home page when they visit the website. If a user has come via a link from a search engine or via a link from another site, they are

Navigation bar: nice and clear this. You know you are on 'Home' and what other sections are on offer. But what happens when you are in a sub-section under portfolio?

likely to land on a page lower down in the navigation. The same answer to the question (Where am I) should apply. At a glance, using primal instinct, is it absolutely obvious where they are? If not, you have failed, my friend.

Aside from highlighting the main section a user has landed in or arrived at during their user journey, you will need to show the path of their journey. Bread crumbs do this job, but in my opinion, if you rely on them then your nav doesn't work properly. Test the site yourself: if you are two sections deep, is it clear which section you are in?

Where have I come from?

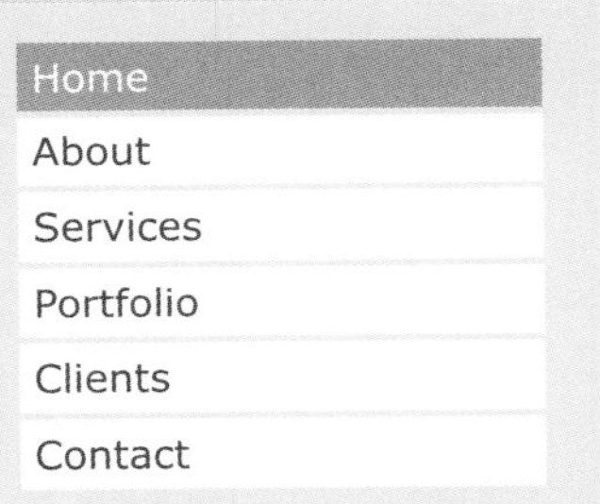

When a user journeys through a site, it is very likely they have gone through various sections and sub-sections. Take this as an example, using a web design agencies' typical navigation.

That just about covers it, right?

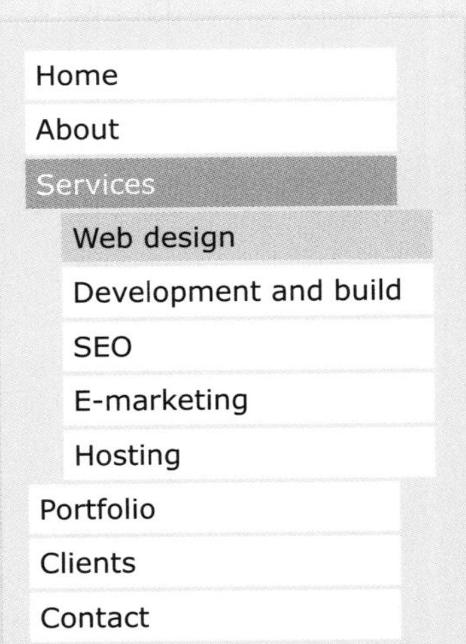

Now consider this, we are in a sub-section of 'Services' called web design using the vertical navigation style.

We could have used pop out dropdowns to reduce the depth of this, but as you will see, that can make things difficult when you have multiple sub-sections.

Let's see what happens when things get a bit more complex.

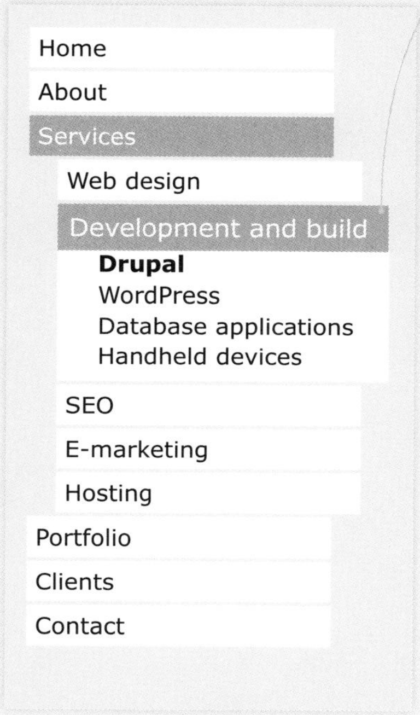

Home
About
Services
Web design
Development and build
Drupal
WordPress
Database applications
Handheld devices
SEO
E-marketing
Hosting
Portfolio
Clients
Contact

Very quickly, the depth of navigation has expanded to three levels on what is a very simple website. People often harp on about the number of clicks to get to content – three often being cited as the maximum. I'm not convinced that this is such a consideration; I think users will happily click as long as they are informed along their journey. However, as you can see from this example for a tiny site for a small agency, very quickly we are three levels down in the navigation.

It ain't pretty: *this is just a diagram, but it does show – now that the navigation is three levels down – that it is increasingly difficult to illustrate 'Where you are' and 'Where you have come from'. We'll make it pretty later.*

So, how does the designer show that the user is on the Drupal page and where that page sits in the preceding sections? Well?

Put it this way, you can't just show the user 'Where am I?' You will need to find a way of indicating, 'where have I come from' as well. Not only that, the design for your navigation system will need to show the 'weight', or importance of each section. In this case, services is top-level, then development and build is the sub-section and Drupal a section under that. Easy peasy, until you have a content structure that is five times this size. Then you really have your work cut out. This work has to be done right at the beginning of the design process, because navigation often defines the very nature of the site.

There are a few things you can use to help users understand the hierarchy of your website navigation and where they are within it. These include:

Weight and style: this means the weight of the type of graphic, i.e. very bold, bold, roman, light, etc.

Colour: for instance, dark blue, blue, mid blue and light blue (often used to show depth).

Position: how high it is in the navigation, in the case of sub-sections, how far it is indented.

Indicator: either using an arrow, pointer or graphic.

Of course, designers more often than not use more than one of these devices at a time, and some crazy maniacs use all of them! Did you spot the potential issue with all of these tricks? When designing a website with a large amount of content, with very deep navigation, you can't go on for ever making things lighter or indenting them even further, it would be ridiculous and, eventually, defeat the object.

With big sites, navigation problems need to be looked at, in the architecture stage, then the designer stands a chance of getting it right and it being right for a reasonable length of time. It is vital to consider the longevity of the structure and style of the navigation.

It is very important to remember that websites grow. New sections get added and new sub-sections will come into play. If you haven't allowed for a level of flexibility in the architecture, it will 'break'. Trying to break your design is a good stage to go through. You'll see what I mean in a bit.

With a lot of CMS driven sites, navigation is referred to as 'parent' and 'child', parent being the main section and child being a sub-section. 'Weight' or 'weighting' refers to how high the link is on the list, in our example, 'About', has a high or heavier weight than 'Services'. Therefore, 'About' appears higher up the list than 'Services'. See what I mean?

The current scope of the site might be defined at this stage, and the client may say "it will never change". Ahem, it most probably will. So take a long hard look at your navigation design and imagine what will happen when three more main sections are added, two sub-sections and...Wait for it, a sub-sub section (tertiary navigation). Can your navigation handle that, or will it suffer a nervous breakdown?

Where can I go?

Bet you thought I'd forgotten about this bit, didn't you? So, I'm sitting there, looking at a web page about what-not, now what? what can I do next? It's important to offer – and sometimes highlight – what else is on offer within each section on a web page. A while ago designers used this technique where navigation would open and close as you moused over. It was a nightmare, the thing used to bounce up and down like mad and you had to time it just right even to have a hope in hell of clicking on the button you wanted. And of course, the navigation was closed, so it wasn't clear what was there, where you were and where you might want to go, without performing this ridiculous dance.

Where possible, keep the navigation section the users are in 'open' and visible, and allow them to see other sections that they might be interested in. You want them to have a good look around, don't you?

In-page navigation

I am really not a fan of this at all. In fact, I feel queasy just mentioning it, but I feel honour-bound not to ignore it, instead do my best to undermine this heinous idea and persuade you to cast out the concept like the navigation maestro you are – or will be.

In-page nav is when the user is in a certain section of the website and the designer introduces a new set of navigation for that section in the page! This new form of navigation does not sit in the main set of navigation, because it either hasn't been accommodated in the design, the client has forced you to do it, or you didn't fix it earlier or try to break it. The problem with in-page nav is what happens when you select a page: where does the rest of the navigation go?

Clients say things like, 'they can click back' or, click on the home page, Oh my life, using the browser back button as an excuse for poor navigation design should be a criminal offence. "What are you in prison for?" "They caught me forcing users to use the back button on the browser".

In-page nav is a result of not understanding the scope of a site, how a user might interact with it, and what the user might want to do next. I'm sorry to say that if at any point in your career you ever get in a place where you even consider this, then know you have failed.

In-page nav is not the same as a call to action. So there.

Number of clicks

The number of clicks refers to the number of times a user has to click to get to a section within a website. Clients like writing in their briefs that no page should be more than three clicks away. OK. But it doesn't always work like that, with dropdowns or 'mega menus' you can go deep into a site with one click or, on the other hand, big e-commerce sites need deeper nav than three clicks. If you get the architecture and the design right, you should be able to circumvent the whole three click thing. It matters, but only sometimes.

Tumblr has no navigation on the landing page at all! You can't even have a poke about without signing in.

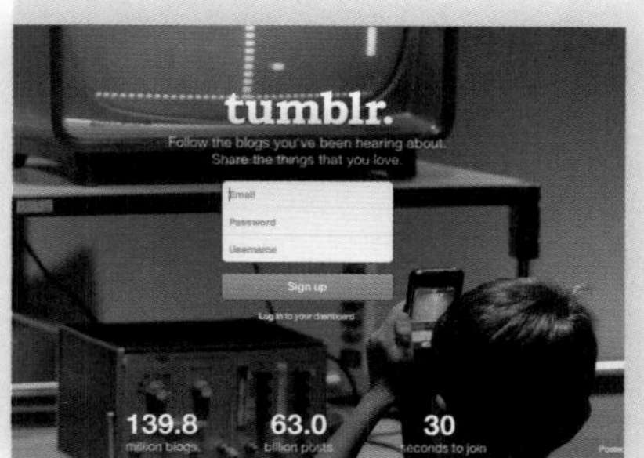

Minimal nav

There has been a movement recently, even on sites with tonnes of content, to distill the top level nav down to the absolute minimum. Jolly good it is too. It is often used on sites when the user is encouraged to explore or browse – what does that mean? Well, it means look about, see what's here and see if you like it. The difference here is that the entire website content couldn't be displayed in a comprehensive navigation system and users don't necessarily know what they are looking for. Things like big photo sites and social media sites use this as a way round what would otherwise be a big problem. So they 'say' to the user, have a look, see what you can find...

Breadcrumbs

Breadcrumbs are like a back-up when nav does not work. Perhaps you know the story: Hansel and Gretel were surfing the internet with a baguette as a way of them leaving a trail behind them to find their way home. They leave breadcrumbs strewn all over the page so that they can find their way home. I think that is the way it goes. Anyway, if the navigation system was designed properly, Hansel and Gretel would clearly be able to tell where they had come from and not feel lost in the first place.

With thanks to the Brothers Grimm for their early navigation advice, circa 1812.

Breadcrumbs are automatically generated by certain CMS and are usually displayed at the top of the page, just above the main content. They only show where you have been and look like this (see right).

HOME > FRUIT > CITRUS > LEMONS

HOME FRUIT CITRUS LEMONS

Way finding: breadcrumbs can be just live text or nicely styled, just like anything else. All you have to do is care.

They are handy because they are clear and often repeated at the bottom of the page as well, but they only serve one purpose: to allow users to click back to the sections they have been in. I would recommend that really they are an unnecessary extra element, just more clutter, but Hansel and Gretel loved them.

Types of navigation

Horizontal navigation

Horizontal navigation is the old hand, the 'anchor man' of navigation styles. A bit stuck in his ways, reliable, but a bit inflexible.

Nearly all sites feature some form of horizontal navigation. Users are used to seeing it, it's usually at the top of the page under the masthead and is very prominent.

All good, then. Except the big problem is, eventually you will run out of space as only so many words can fit across the horizontal width. Even when your client says there definitely won't be any more top level buttons, so horizontal nav is fine, you can bet, down the line that will change and you will be left with trying to squeeze in extra words, making type smaller and trying all sorts of twisting and turning to get it to fit in.

There are some very big sites out there that suffer from this problem. There are also some hideous solutions people have tried to implement to fix the problem. And I can understand why. As a web designer you really need to grasp this and get it right.

The tab system is still a favourite – nothing wrong with tabs, they highlight the section you are in nicely and people can reminisce about ring binders and dividers, when filing was real filing. Everything gets a bit clumsy when you want to use horizontal navigation with a sub-horizontal navigation. When using tabs, and here comes that problem again, you only have so much space you can use. And if you have a tertiary set of navigation, oh my life, what a pickle. It becomes incredibly difficult to fix: it can be done, but it is hard to get right.

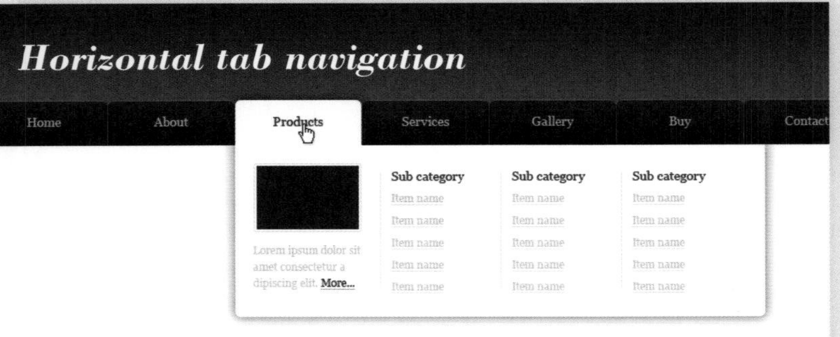

This shows a tab style that uses horizontal navigation with mega menu dropdowns. Note there is space for embedding an image. Here's one for you: if the user clicks on one of the items, how will you show where they are in the navigation?

The challenge here is to, if needs be, link the horizontal nav with a second set of navigation. I think there are two ways of doing this, you can either link it visually to a left hand nav, or use dropdowns.

Dropdowns

Dropdowns solve a few problems: they give a nice easy way to allow users to access sections under the top level navigation, and they can even allow users to access sub-sub navigation. Dropdowns can be tiny, little neat jobs, or great big panels that are often called 'mega menus'.

There are a couple of things to bear in mind here – mega menus can obscure the content below or behind, although that may not matter. They can also cause problems on small handheld devices, and of course, they don't fix every navigational problem. When using dropdowns on a site with lots of sections it becomes unmanageable: at best they fix a second level, or sub-nav level problem. They give the user direct access to sub-nav and occasionally third level nav, which is handy.

I've seen mega menus hold images and even video to indicate the glorious content that follows. They then start to be pages themselves – I'm not convinced.

The other thing about them is that they cannot clearly show a user's path. Because they close themselves, they cannot show you where you are. If you select say, 'Services' and then 'Web design', when you are happily looking at examples of fabulous web design, dropdowns don't show where you have come from and where you are.

They do give users direct access to deep content, they help avoid scrolling and help the information architects to pack in a ton of content into a relatively small space.

Dropdowns can be implemented with left hand navigation (they are sometimes called pop out menus) and again, more than two levels of navigation can be implemented. There's a thing called 'mouse out' where the developer codes the area that makes the menu 'pop out'. Have you ever been in the situation where you are trying to select a sub-section in a pop out or dropdown menu and you can't get the thing to stay open long enough to click on the link? That's a mouse out problem.

Don't forget that users may click on the top level link in the nav – the link that, on mouse over, pops out the dropdowns – so you will need to make sure that some content appears on this page. In our example that would be 'Services'. If you decide you don't want content on the Services button, then when the user does click, the dropdown should be activated.

***Top level:** what happens when the user just clicks on 'Phones'? Do they go to a page about phones or does it just activate the pop out menu?*

This problem can be fixed using jQuery code that tracks the path of the user's mouse.

Horizontal navigation and left hand navigation

I would suggest that this combination is probably the most successful double act in the navigation cabaret. Whilst the horizontal navigation serves its usual purpose, to highlight, the left hand nav comes into play and delivers the second, third and, on occasion, fourth levels. And does it well.

A visual link between the selected section and the section type in the left hand navigation needs to be made. In our case, it might look something like this.

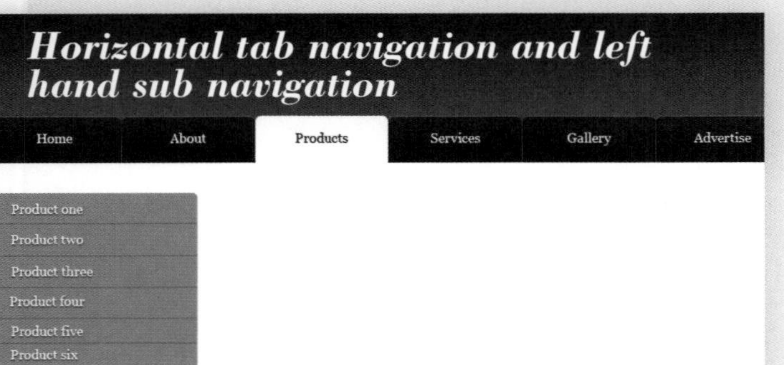

You can see that this team does a great job together when you, the designer, need to deal with lots of sections and sub-sections. The depth of the left hand navigation is relatively short, as sub-sections are only open when you are in them.

On websites with horrific amounts of content, these left hand navigation panels actually change entirely to accommodate entirely new sets of navigation for the section they are in. I don't think I will win a 'Plain English' award for that sentence, so I will illustrate it here.

Left hand only navigation

Some sites do away with old faithful, Lord Horizontal of Nav, and go it alone with just the left hand nav. I've seen this really work and I've also seen it look a bit odd and heavy handed sitting there on its own: so the design and style comes into play here.

Certainly, the positive side of just using a left hand nav and nothing else is that it does away with a lot of the issues designers have linking horizontal nav and all that hoo-haa.

You do have to be careful with the depth of the navigation panel so that it doesn't get out of control and finish up so far down the page the users have to scroll 2000 leagues under the sea to get to the bottom.

Sometimes it helps to see what not to do, like the example shown right that I bought from a template site.

What's wrong with this? This bar could be about a third shorter just by removing a few pixels from each bar. Do you really need those little symbols? And you know how I feel about icons...

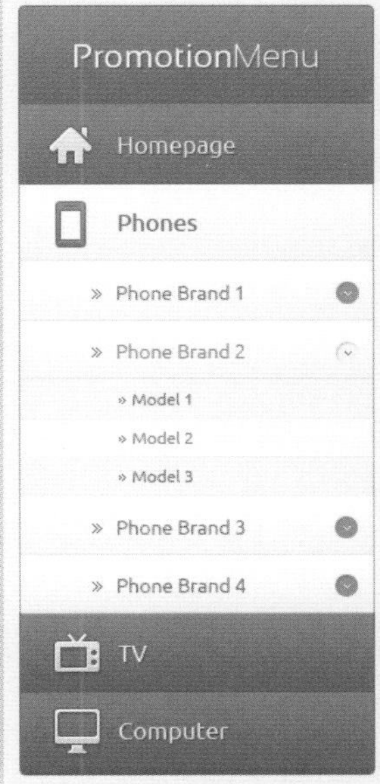

Using a kite to comb your hair

Using the right tool for the right job can save you time, energy, repayments on your mortgage and hair loss. I know. I lost my hair years ago. Despite the software companies telling you that you can use a well-known writing program to author websites – you would be bonkers to try. You can use Illustrator to design websites, but Photoshop is far better. It is the best and, despite there being oodles of alternatives around in my experience, nothing beats it.

For wire framing, use any of the online tools: whichever you feel comfortable with. Wireframes are the ugly ducklings of web design, so ease of use and functionality should be your main considerations. I reckon Axure is your best bet.

Photoshop comes with an animated gif building function which is good. But again, there are plenty of free online tools.

Think about the right program to use for the right task, don't just use what you are used to because it is the easy option. Learn the experts' tools if you want to be an expert. See 'What app to use and when', page 54.

SHOW ME THE WAY HOME:

- Navigation is one of the most important considerations in your web design; give it the attention it deserves.
- Remember the future is uncertain, you must allow for your navigation to grow, even if you are told it won't.
- Use design to clearly show, 'Where am I?', 'Where have I come from?' and 'Where can I go?'

THE PRINCIPLES OF GOOD BUILD

Proper code

This book is not about code. But somebody has to check that the code they get from the developer is good. And 'good' can mean a lot of things, this is not a black and white issue. There are a hundred different ways to skin a cat and there are a hundred different ways to code something. So, good code is subject to opinion to a certain extent.

There are a couple of things I suggest you ask for and look for in the code that is supplied. First of all, run the website through a validator. W3C, the snappy spy sounding organisation that defends the world against bad code, offer a free service that will check your code. You can find it here: http://validator.w3.org

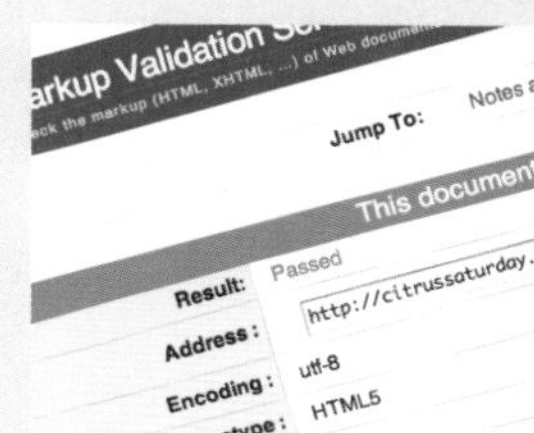

Pass: this is what you should be aiming for.

The second basic thing is to make sure the developer comments his code. These are little notes that get typed into the code, with slashes and asterisks that hide the code from the browser. They explain what the developer is doing or the purpose of that particular part of the code. Who cares? Well, if the website is to be picked up at a later date by another developer, these clues help them understand what the hell is going on. If you can be bothered, right click on a web page and view the source. Nine times out of ten you will see the comments and nine times out of ten they won't make sense to you.

Accessibility

This relates to how a website is designed and coded to allow all types of users to be able to use it. W3C, our validator pals, have a programme called WAI, which stands for the Web Accessibility Initiative. This lays out the principles and subsequent accreditation for websites to help designers and coders build websites for everyone.

Accessibility issues:
Page title
Image text
Headings
Colour contrast
Zoom
Keyboard access
Form fields
Video and audio alternatives
Plain content view

Accessibility covers a wide range of things, from the design of the interface, the contrast of the colours, to code that helps people who are blind use the internet with their screen

W3C WAI-AA WCAG 2.0

Old medals: there was a time when displaying your accreditation medals at the bottom of your site was highly desirable, these days you don't see them.

W3C VALIDATOR Suite

How suite: W3C have launched a service that gathers up these validation services here: validator-suite.w3.org.

W3C Semantic Web

All together now: a consortium of jolly good people working towards a new standard for the way we use the web.

readers. These conventions enable people with disabilities to have access to your site rather than exclude them.

Accreditation comes in three flavours: A, AA, AAA. Under most circumstances, websites aim for AA (not to be confused with batteries). Read up on it (http://www.w3.org/WAI/) so you know what's what. If it comes up in a meeting, you need to understand the principles and know what design guides are in place to ensure the world can use your site. Make sure your developer knows from day one the level of accreditation you require and if the client asks for AAA, then you really need to know your onions. After all, why would you exclude anyone?

Languages

I'm opening a tin of worms here, and when I open it, I peer inside and can only really identify a few of the worms.

To the designer, to a certain extent, who cares how it's coded and what language the developer uses, right? Right. But like I've said, whilst you do not need to know how to code, it does help when people say things like 'Linux' and you don't confuse that with a luxury car brand or soap. Actually, I like the idea of Linux soap, a soap developed by the people, the recipe is free to download and you could develop your own soap, refining it and releasing it to other soap enthusiasts.

My tin of worms could include so many different worms that we'd be here all day. So all I am prepared to classify are the big worms and leave the rest to the specialists.

HTML: stands for HyperText Markup Language and is the foundation of the vast majority of web pages.

XHTML: the adult version requiring an 18 certificate. Not really. XHTML is part of XML, which is kind of an extension of HTML, like HTML with knobs on. It enables the code to talk to the browser amongst other things in a more expressive way.

HTML5: the new standard that offers a whole heap of different innovation and technical potential, as I mentioned earlier. Older browsers will not support some of the functions. Test, test, test. Always offer an alternative solution for people using older technology.

CSS (Cascading Style Sheets): code that controls the way the page looks in combination with one of the HTML brothers.

PHP: stands for Hypertext Preprocessor. This is possibly the most useless fact in the book and is a language developed by Rasmus Lerdorf, who absolutely sounds like a spy. But he isn't. His language is used by millions of people to code their websites. It's open source and, as a general rule, a PHP developer is cheaper than an ASP developer and a bit more friendly.

ASP.NET: stands for Active Server Pages. Blah. This language was developed by Microsoft, who may sue me for even mentioning their name. It used to be just ASP, then ASPdotNET, then dotNet. I dunno. It is a language for developing websites developed by Bill Gates' mates and is a language that helps developers create dynamic web pages that are connected to a database. It is the direct competitor to PHP.

Java: a program language with a nice aroma and is served in small cups. Actually, it is a language that gets used to create things like games.

JavaScript: a programming language that can be inserted into HTML and therefore makes the code actually 'do' something. It should not be confused with Java.

jQuery: adds functionality to a site using scripts. Carousels and image galleries for instance.

Action script: the language that Flash uses to add functionality to the animations.

I don't know about you, I'm bored of this now, so I suggest as you go along, you ask the developer why he chooses one language over another. If in doubt and you have an inquisitive nature, look it up.

Twitter's Bootstrap, there are others out there.

Principles of cross platform build

Browsers

It's vital that all the websites that get built for your clients are tested in multiple environments. Unless you have hundreds of computers in your office, you will need to use a render engine. These online tools process the code and display how the website will look, so you can check as many devices as you like. Just search for 'cross browser testing'.

Bootstrap grid examples

Basic grid layouts to get you familiar with building within the Bootstrap grid system.

Three equal columns

Get three equal-width columns **starting at desktops and scaling to large desktops**. On mobile devices, tablets and below, the columns will automatically stack.

.col-md-4 .col-md-4 .col-md-4

Three unequal columns

Get three columns **starting at desktops and scaling to large desktops** of various widths. Remember, grid columns should add up to twelve for a single horizontal block. More than that, and columns start stacking no matter the viewport.

.col-md-3 .col-md-6 .col-md-3

Two columns

Get two columns **starting at desktops and scaling to large desktops**.

.col-md-8 .col-md-4

Full width, single column

Bootstrap grid examples

Basic grid layouts to get you familiar with building within the Bootstrap grid system.

Three equal columns

Get three equal-width columns **starting at desktops and scaling to large desktops**. On mobile devices, tablets and below, the columns will automatically stack.

.col-md-4

.col-md-4

.col-md-4

Three unequal columns

Get three columns **starting at desktops and scaling to large desktops** of various widths. Remember, grid columns should add up to twelve for a single horizontal block. More than that, and columns start stacking no matter the viewport.

.col-md-3

.col-md-6

.col-md-3

Bootstrap

Those chaps at Twitter have developed a framework of code elements that comes in jolly handy for developers to work from. Basically, the system is a collection of code for typical website elements that can be customised to match your designs. Don't worry, this isn't a theme, it is just code that offers really handy starting points, like the responsive grid (see left).

The difference between responsive and adaptive

Both of these terms refer to the problem of rendering on a wide and ever widening range of devices. They both aim to fix the problem – just in a slightly different way. I'll explain.

Responsive delivers the elements within the website in a flexible way, they change size and shape depending on what you view them on.

Adaptive delivers the same content, but in predefined sizes to suit the device you are viewing it on. In effect there are different sets of code sitting there waiting to be presented to the device (and screen size) they were designed for. Get it?

Transform gracefully/Graceful degradation
This is a principle and a principle that you should try to apply to any and every web experience you design and ultimately build. The aim is to deliver a similar user experience, no matter what device the user is using. The idea is that the older the technology, the more limited the features you may have at your disposal. If you use Google on your phone, you will see that it works just great, but not all the features are there and its interface has not 'responded' to the device.

A word on SEO

As I begin to write this sentence I can tell you what I think is the basic principles of search engine optimisation (SEO), but by the time I get to the end, it will most likely be out of date.

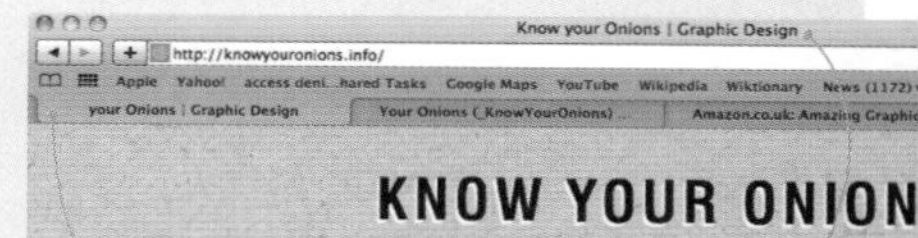

The right title: these are the page titles, that are added into the pages when they are built.

So try as I might, this will be in no way comprehensive and the technology will rapidly change. But here goes. The page title of your website (the one that appears in the browser bar) is important, so it needs to be named to match the content and search terms you are aiming at. If you look at the code of a website, you will see what is called the meta data, here lives the description and key words. The search engines will read these and the content and then figure out if this page fits the search.

The amount of other websites that link to your site will help with SEO. The search engines reckon that if a lot of people think your content has a lot of links to it, it must be good.

Search engines also take a look at the content in the pages themselves and add importance to it in varying degrees. For instance, the H1 tag (the headline tag) is quite important. What does this matter to the designer? Well, you should learn the basics at the very least and then, when applying your design, you might consider not using a graphic for the headline, which the search engine cannot read, and use nicely styled live text instead.

Google does what it calls a 'dance' every now and then and changes its mind on what's important and what's not. It's a full-time job keeping up.

DESIGNING FOR A CONTENT MANAGEMENT SYSTEM

Designing a website that is going to be built in PHP, ASP or just HTML and CSS should make no difference to you one way or the other. The same applies with what Content Management Systems (CMS) or blogging software the website will end up using or being built by. However, all good artists and designers should understand and master their materials – and that means you.

During the design process detailed above, I mentioned a time when it might be wise to go and have a chat with the developer. At that point you should be asking them to highlight anything that is going to be a nightmare to build and update. Building and updating are two different issues, but intrinsically linked.

I promised you that this book was not a technical book. And I will honour that promise. Like driving a car, it's good to know what the clutch and gearbox does, but you don't need to know how to build one to drive one. Same applies here.

First of all, I'll try to explain how some CMSs came about and how most work, and then I'll cover some of the things to bear in mind when designing for one.

Where does all this CMS come from?

At Navig8, our preferred CMS is Drupal. It is mega powerful, the community that supports it is huge, and there is not much that we ask it to do that it can't. There are literally hundreds of CMS systems out there. Another popular one is called Joomla. Both Joomla and Drupal are 'open source'. Open source code gives me faith in humanity. Basically, somebody spent their own time and, for no direct financial gain, developed a system. Once they had finished it, they allowed anybody who wants it to download and install it for free. Brilliant. These people 'release the code' into the 'community' and other people develop the system even further. They in turn release the code and the system develops and grows. It takes on a life of its own.

Top 3 CMS:

Drupal: drupal.org

Joomla: joomla.org

Wordress: wordpress.com

Every now and then a new version of the system is released and the community sets about developing code, patches and little modules of functionality. What is amazing is that if our developer has an issue installing a module, he goes online and chats with other developers all over the world and they help each other. They don't even buy each other a pint to say 'thank you'. Our developer, in turn, will help someone else and release his custom modules into the community. This kind of global relationship is a big and world-changing outcome, enabled by the internet.

Then they all get together around a virtual bonfire and someone gets out an acoustic guitar and they sing songs about code they used to know, or tell IT themed jokes: "Once I was a coder, I was petrified, I knew I could never live with ASP by my side, but then I spent so many nights with PHP..." In true anti-capitalist style these software platforms have performed their own coup and taken a lot of power from the giant software dictatorships. The masterminds behind these mini revolutions become respected and revered, a bit like Che Guevara, but with fewer cigars.

Other spirited people have gone on and developed huge websites in this manner, like Wikipedia, or browsers like Firefox, or even complete operating systems like Linux. Trust me, this is an amazing movement and worthy of your respect. If you get an opportunity to give something back – do it.

Some developers and web design agencies build their own systems, sometimes they are referred to as proprietary systems, because you have to pay to use them, and of course there are a stack of systems that you can buy. Blah.

How do most of them work?

I can't cover everything and explain how every CMS works because A: I don't know everything and B: this book would be so insanely dull if I did. So I'll stick to what I know and what I think you need to know. I cover a bit more in 'How it all fits together', which is full of diagrams and will make people who like PowerPoint very happy.

This bit is useful to know, you'll have to trust me.

CMSs treat content, words and some images as one thing and functionality as another – this is a principle, read it again. They kind of separate the component parts of a website out. They do this so that they can manage the content and let the users edit it, serve it on a page or pages, all from one central store. That store is called a database.

When you click on a link and a web page loads into your browser window, the code reads the content from the database and pops it into the page. The code then says, "This is where I want it to be on the page and I want it to look like this.". Code is very chatty. In the split second it's taken to load a web page, the code has had a conversation with your browser, made a number of requests to the database and it has flirted with the host. That is why a web page with lots of functionality and content can take time for the page to finish loading, especially if you have a slow internet connection.

If you can try and remember that – when designing for a CMS – all the editable content in the web page you are designing is stored away from the page itself, it will help you in the future. 'Static' sites don't work that way, but for now, we are talking about what are called 'dynamic' sites.

When your content managed site is built, the developer can choose to allow content to be editable or not. This is called setting permissions and most systems allow for more than one level of permission.

In the case of Drupal, the various modules that have been chosen and installed control the functionality. For instance, you might want a forum on your site. The system will shove all the comments and questions into the database and the forum module will enable users to post topics and questions, as well as allow them to ask stupid things, be rude and use way too many exclamation marks!

When all this is done, the system applies a theme. A theme controls how it looks.

Content: *words, pictures, video etc, stored in the database*

+

Module: *functionality is implemented*

+

Theme: *the content is arranged and styled*

=

Serve: *the page and content is combined and served in the browser*

Modules: *a bit like plug-ins, they control the functionality of the site, for instance 'sign up'. There are over 23,000 modules out there at the moment.*

What is a theme?

When we design for CMS or blogging systems like WordPress, the way the site looks is controlled by a theme. You will probably know that you can download free themes for WordPress and apply them to your site (the same applies to systems like Tumblr). You can change the theme, but the content doesn't change. Again, that's because the system treats the two things separately – content is separate from the way it is displayed.

A theme consists of a number of things and the extent of those things will depend on how many elements within your site you need to style. Themes are controlled by styles and graphics. The styles sit in a bit of code, called the CSS file or the theme. Most of the time, the CSS sits on its own on the server like a French impressionist artist, smoking Galoise and waiting to turn boring old content into something magnifique!

The good thing about CSS is that one tiny bit of code controls the way the whole thing looks. It does this site-wide, so if you are not happy with the way your headlines look, you can ask the developer to tweak the code and the new style gets applied across the whole site. If you have a friendly developer, you can make these tweaks sitting next to them and they upload the CSS file, refresh the browser and see the results. You can sit there all day changing your mind and getting them to cater for your every whim, but they may punch you.

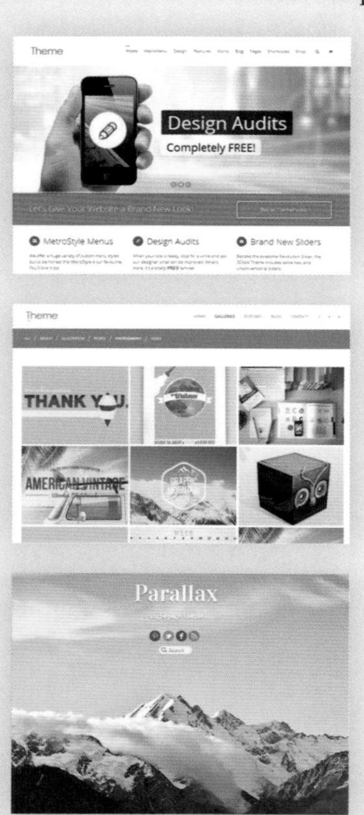

Above: these WordPress themes display the content differently. Some are free, some you pay for.

As a general rule, you can style just about any element of the site, from the form fields to the borders of a box. Styling some things can make the developer's life tricky and usually those trickier things are the things that cause compatibility problems with different browsers.

The big issue is this, and learn it well, text. What we call 'live text' is editable and style-able using the theme. But once you start using graphics, pictures of text for instance, that have been exported from Photoshop, then these cannot be edited. As a designer, you will want everything to look just so. Therefore you will want to use graphics so the site looks as you intended it to. After all, graphics look the same, or pretty much the same, no matter what you view them on.

I suggest you use graphics with care, especially when it comes to making text a graphic. There are ways round it to get a brilliant looking site without making it 'graphic heavy'.

That means you can take the content of any website to look any way you want, what great larks you can have taking your accountant's site and styling it for a rap artist.

The great thing about themes is that you can have multiple installations of a website, or even just one, and apply different themes. So get this: you can load a theme as a user enters the site and if they select a certain section within the site, the system can load an entirely different theme.

Don't underestimate how long it takes a developer to theme a site. It takes a long time to do it properly. Take into consideration that once it has been built and looks lovely on his screen, he'll have to fiddle around for you to get it looking OK on all other browsers.

What to bear in mind when designing for a CMS

The whole point of the CMS is to allow users, your clients, to edit and update the site themselves. So you have to think about these editable areas and design them so that the elements can be edited. This sounds so stupid, I know, but it really is a common mistake. I'll give you a for instance. If the system allows users to add pages and sub-pages into the navigation, you can't make those buttons graphics. You can make the background of the button a graphic, so that it looks like a nice rounded button, but the text that says what the button is, like 'Contact Us' must be live text.

The background graphic is the red lozenge, the text is 'live', i.e. editable as opposed to making it part of the image itself.

Of course, this only applies to sites which you are designing that allow users to update. If you are designing a static site, then the client is going to be coming back to you to add in the new page and you will generate a new button and the developer will add it into the navigation.

What is a static site?

Before I define static, I'll define the opposite, dynamic. Dynamic sites are sites that draw in content from a database or an external source. A static site has all the content in the page. The words sit and live within the HTML pages themselves. Going back to our accountant's site, if they decide not to opt for any of your 'What ifs', then the site probably doesn't do anything. They will contact you when one of the partners kicks the bucket and you or the developer will make the changes.

When I'm having an initial chat with a client, I'll discuss updates and gauge the level of changes they might make in a month. Clients know that a fully working CMS site costs more from the start, but then they don't need to pay for updates. But if it is likely they will want to do regular updates, then a static site will make things expensive.

How on earth are you going to fit 'entrepreneur's recourses' in this horizontal navigation bar?

You are not a developer. Or perhaps you are and you are reading this to learn design. But it can be a surprise to both the designer and the client – what may appear a simple change to a website can involve an enormous amount of work. I'll give you a for instance. For instance, if you have eight buttons, beautifully spaced across a horizontal navigation bar and the client decides that they want to add two more saying 'Promotional offers' and Entrepreneur's recourses' then it is unlikely that they will fit in the width. This happens a lot with horizontal navigation; try to put too much in there and you run out of space. The whole navigation bar will not only have to be redesigned, but also rebuilt. Watch out for horizontal navigation bars!

The principles of applying brand

Again, I have to make assumptions as to your situation. I'll assume that you have been briefed to design a website for a company that has a logo and the bare bones of a corporate identity. Perhaps they have been using you and your agency to design their brochures and stationery. These brand elements will underpin your designs styles, or at least they should. Web design is not like design for print, you can incorporate some brand elements but there are certain requirements a website has that won't be covered in the typical design suite. A lot of bigger companies have brand guidelines, and some tackle online styles. What is normally covered are RGB colour conversions of the corporate colour palette and 'web safe' fonts. If the brand guidelines are more extensive than that, then your work is cut out for you, and all you need to do is read it carefully and apply the styles. More often than not, this is not the case.

You need to take a view of your client's brand and get to know it. Remember, brand is not just the colours and type styles. If you are working for a quirky cool brand, then you can design your site to be quirky and cool. That might mean the dropdowns in the navigation pop out in an unusual way, or the graphics adopt a certain texture.

If you look at a site like Apple computers, the brand and style complements their product range beautifully. It's not the same – it just feels like it belongs. And that is your mission.

If you've been designing an annual report, it is unlikely the printed material will have buttons, because buttons don't work on the printed page. Buttons, as we know, change state, they change colour or style when you roll over them or when you have clicked them. This example is one tiny instance, but you can see there is more scope and more to consider when applying a brand to a website. There are loads of instances in web design that create new considerations when applying brand, some of which, as the designer, you will create yourself.

You are tackling something that is interactive – it does something. I've gone on about a thing called an elements page; a page that isn't real but defines the style site-wide. But the brand issue is much more top level than that.

Below are some things that spring to mind when considering brand. We touched on some of these when we were talking about the website for the band (careful reading required,

Stylish: three pages from three style guides covering logo positioning, colour palette and font use.

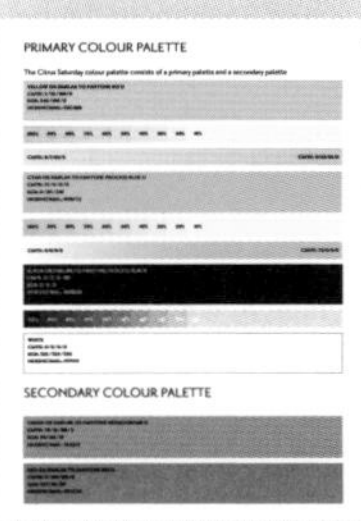

My definition of brand: the manifestation of a person, organisation or product communicating its essence, activity, aspirations and personality.

brand and band). What you need to do is make your design appropriate to the brand.

Think about:

- Will you need other colours adding to the palette to ensure you have enough for all of the rollover and visited states?
- What fonts will you need for all of the headlines, body text and any other bits of content? Are there web safe versions that will work?
- How should the images be treated in terms of style and crop?
- What if the images move or animate - how should the transitions work?
- Does your client use short, snappy headlines or are they more descriptive? That will affect the length of them; maybe the headlines will run to three lines.
- What level of typographic hierarchy will the content need?
- Think about their tone of voice.

I've seen designers create a website for a client based on one of the company's leaflets: it just doesn't work, how can it? It is an entirely different medium.

Typography

If you are a print designer, it is likely that you will have a passion for typography, or at the very least, if not a passion you might fancy a bit of tight kerning. Print designers can sit around all day choosing from millions of fonts and carefully placing type on page.

Web designs don't have that luxury. You have to get over this very early on and work with what's out there. I'll explain.

When your web page gets rendered in the browser, the CSS file tells the browser what font to use. Remember the little CSS file? It will say, "Make this bit of text Helvetica, 18 pixels and blue.". And the viewer's browser will use the version of Helvetica installed on the viewer's computer and display the text in the right font.

But, what happens if the viewer's computer doesn't have Helvetica (or Arial) loaded? In the case of Helvetica, the likelihood of the font not being installed is very low. But if the designer had specified Priory Sans, the story would be very different.

Priory Sans light
Priory Sans regular
Priory Sans bold

When dealing with live text, the designers and developers must specify what are called 'web safe fonts'. These are:

Arial
Helvetica
Verdana
Georgia
Times

Just my type: the fonts typeset here are all 24pt and all 'web safe'. Note: Arial and Helvetica are almost identical. Verdana and Georgia are the only ones that were designed for screen use.

Times is the default font. So, if you haven't specified a font, it will be Times as the browser reads your page. These are called 'web safe' because it's safe to say that all (well, almost all) computers will have these fonts installed when they come out of the box.

When developers code your font style in that hard-working little CSS file, it will say, "This bit of text should be in Verdana, if you don't have Verdana, then style it Helvetica, if you don't have Helvetica, then use Arial.". What it should say next is, "If you don't have Arial, you live in a cave.".

Arial is Microsoft's version of Helvetica. It is very, very similar, but generally recognised as not quite as good.

Verdana (designed by Mathew Carter for Microsoft in 1996, as was Georgia) is a web safe font to be designed specifically for screen use. It renders really well at small sizes, where as Times does not. But then it was never designed to.

Georgia has become popular recently as designers try to move on from sans serifs and search for a serif that still looks good on screen. For a 90's kid, it has been a slow burner. Again, designed for screen use, it displays really well at all sizes and looks jolly nice italicised.

TIP:

Colour your type a dark grey rather than black, it makes it just a bit easier on the eye without affecting the legibility.

@font-face

Font replacement: above are three different font replacement services. Don't use font replacement on large areas of text, use sparingly for headlines and such.

As things change in the world of the web, and change at a very quick pace they do, more and more fonts get added to the web safe palette. Both HTML and CSS come in versions and as these versions get higher, more and more things can be done. So that's your tool kit when it comes to fonts. It is remarkable what you can do with such a small suite.

There are some third party font systems that enable you to choose any font you like, and have them display on any website you like and any time you like – except the technology just isn't quite there yet (as I write). Cufón allows you to use any font, but the render isn't perfect (what is?) and the ability to select the type in the page isn't quite there. But it is a big step (and there are others out there) in helping designers get a better and truer type rendition that gives you more creative scope when it comes to typography. Talk to your developer and watch them roll their eyes as you discuss your 'i's.

Measurements with type

Type is measured in points, the same way it is in print design. And points are relative. A point in one font is not the same in another font, it is relative.

Try this: type in your favourite word in 18pt. Select, say, Times as your typeface. Type in the same word again in 18pt and change the typeface to Helvetica. Even though both fonts are 18pt, they appear different sizes. Type sizes are not fixed sizes (yikes), they all vary. Some typefaces look massive at 12pt, others look small. You can see this on the previous page, but try it for yourself.

When developers code your type sizes they use a variety of ways (declarations), see below.

Pixel (px): Pixels are fixed sizes representing one pixel per dot which can be used to recreate a more accurate representation of design.

EM (em): Is equal to the current font size, for example if the current size of the document is 14px then 2em would be 24px.

Per cent (%): Same as em percent is relative, for example if the parent element is 12px 50% of it would be 6px.

Point (pt): Points are generally used in print CSS. Since points are used in print design, the point is used in Print CSS to accurately print the right size.

The other ways of declaring font sizes are small, x-small, xx-small, medium, large, x-large and xx-large.

Type that has a size specified in % will make it fully scalable for mobile devices and it is good practice for accessibility. Specifying in pixels has the advantage of recreating the design on screen more faithfully, but of course the drawback is that it won't scale in mobile devices. Like all things web, there is a compromise somewhere or other.

Eh?: print CSS? Well, some sites have a special CSS file to render content so that when the user presses 'print', it loads the custom CSS and the text looks great when it shuffles out of the printer.

Spacing with type

You can control spacing with type in your designs. But the controls are not as refined as in print design, and the display changes depending on browser compatibility.

It is possible to specify the leading spaces after a paragraph return and even the letter spacing. Paragraphs, as we know, are separated by a paragraph return and the obvious choice is to whack in another paragraph return to separate the paragraphs. That's OK. But 'God is in the details' and type reads and looks better with a smaller space, and to achieve that, you will need to specify the space and get the developer to code it.

JUST MY TYPE:

- Choose no more than two typefaces, to be honest one will do most of the time.
- Keep different type sizes to a minimum, 3 or 4 usually cover most scenarios.
- Colouring up text generally looks amateur.

- A paragraph space should not be a whole line space, it should be less, see above – looks horrid.

KNOWLEDGE OF CONVENTIONS

Everywhere, all over the world, things comply with conventions. People are stereotypes, good manners are universal. You can fight against them, ignore them, whatever you choose. But you must understand them first, then you can do what you like.

Conventions do not, in any way, stifle creativity. Cars have four wheels, lights brighten a dark room and chairs are for sitting on (unless you are a lion tamer). Some of the greatest designs this world has seen have been borne out of convention (and intuition) and redefined creativity.

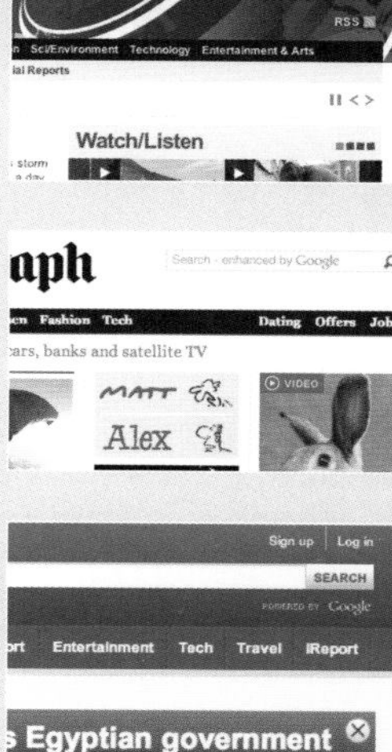

No need to search: above shows the BBC, Telegraph *and CNN websites, all with the search bar top right. If you click on the logo of each of these websites, it links to home. Just two examples of website conventions.*

Logo as home

The company logo or the name of the site – the thing at the top that says what the site is – should always link to the home page. People just expect it to, so make sure you specify that all the time.

Home

Despite the previous paragraph, there still needs to be a home page. And a home button. It needs to say 'Home'. No other term will do, so don't bother trying anything else. The home button should be positioned in the top level navigation, as the first item. Whether you are using a horizontal navigation or a left hand navigation, home usually lives top left, right in the 'Hot Zone' (see page 72).

Search

Search bars are usually positioned top right, perhaps at the end of the horizontal nav bar, or maybe above it. You do see search bars all over the place, but generally this is where people expect them to be, unless the main function of your site is searching, then you can put it slap bang in the middle.

Pay attention: this bit is important.

A point on search as a function. Don't put search engines on sites that don't need them. It looks stupid when the results come back with either nothing or just the one result. It's best to only use them on sites with a large amount of content. Never, ever, ever assume that search can replace navigation. This is an important distinction: searches are for people who know what they are looking for. Navigation shows users what's on the site and enables them to explore.

Login/logout

Like search, login and logout links are what we call site 'utilities'. They are not a direct function of the site, i.e. to sell trousers, but you might need to log into the site to see where those pantaloons have got to.

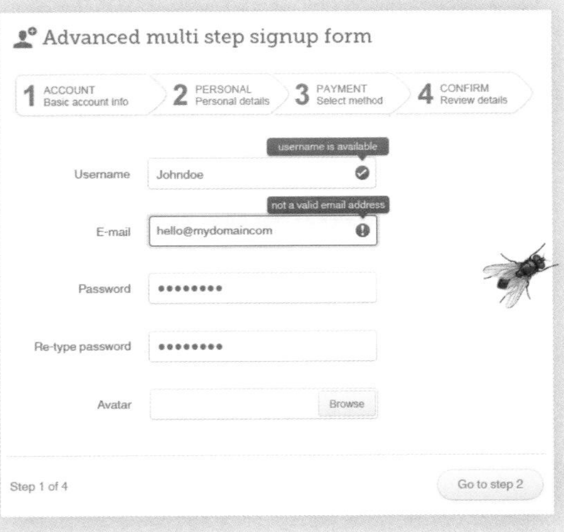

So top right please: it can go very top right as a text link if you like. Do not confuse login with sign up. Sign up is a call to action. Most sites want their users to sign up, so the sign up link tends to be prominent.

Sign up

Whether you are asking your users to sign up for a newsletter or sign up to create an account, they expect certain things. First of all, nobody wants to fill in huge forms with lots of fields. If all you want your users to do is sign up to a newsletter, then take their first name, surname and email. If you are a company that can send a timed offer then it is a good idea to take their birthday and month (don't ask for the year as people get grumpy and feel old if they have to give their year of birth).

Bigger forms need to look short, even if they are not. There are ways of doing this by using two columns, form labels within form fields, and keeping this very 'light' on the eye.

Clear as a bell: this multi-step form is clear, does not look too daunting, even though there is a lot to fill in and gives on the fly prompts.

In terms of functionality, make sure the dev team know that hitting tab on the keyboard moves the cursor to the next field. A lot of users do this and they get jolly ratty if a form isn't built to enable this.

Links

Links can be all manner of things: pictures, headlines – all sorts. Particularly links within text, it really helps if they have an underline. An underline is sometimes better than a change in colour because a change in colour can affect the flow when reading. Links are the life blood of every site. So pay attention to them, make them clear. They should also have a number of states, see right.

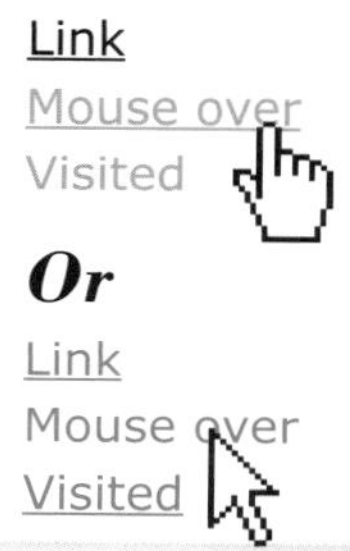

Link up: don't forget to consider all the links styles you will need.

Rollover states

Rollover states are a visual change in something that helps the user understand that it is a link. This can be shown in a number of different ways, but the key thing is to make sure the implementation is consistent. If a link changes colour, has an underline that hides on rollover (also called mouse over), or a combination, make sure it is consistent.

Highlighted states

Stating the obvious is a speciality of mine. Always colour up in the navigation the section you are in, always. If you use tabs, make the tab you are on come to the foreground and make it a different shade or colour.

Clickable items

People expect some elements in a web page to be 'clickable' links. For instance, on a news listing page that shows an image and synopsis of the full news item, users will expect the image and the headline (at least) to link to the main article. Links to other websites should work: most of the time these links open in another window. This helps the user return to the main site without using the dreaded back button. The logos of sponsors or partners tend to link to their own sites, and once again, will open in a new window.

Clickable: when I say 'work', I mean they should not just read as the address, they must also link to the website itself.

Don't make me think: back in about 2000 a chap wrote a book called, Don't Make Me Think, *as it says on the cover 'A Common Sense Approach to Web Usability'. It was very good then and still is today.*

Click here and read more

As a rule of thumb, if an article of synopsis needs 'click here to read more' or something similar, then your links are not clear enough in the content.You should avoid this at all costs. Aside from anything, it looks naff.

Ts&Cs

Ts&Cs (or terms and conditions), privacy policies and the copyright line all go at the bottom of the page, in the footer, as the very last thing. Most of the time range left. Nobody reads them.

Footers

Live at the bottom of the page and should have all of the main links in the site, as well as the copyright statement, Ts&Cs and privacy statements. Every site, almost without exception, should have a footer.They help with navigation, if people are scrolling down as well as with SEO.

Typographic hierarchy

Once you have designed your typographic styles and colour palette, be consistent throughout the whole site and stick to your hierarchy and never, ever change it. If you get to a page or section and the styles on your elements page don't fit with a content type you need, then you have got your elements page wrong.

TREAT THEM WITH RESPECT:

- You may not like the idea of following convention, but your punters will.
- If you want someone to click something, make it visually clear it is clickable.
- Keep link styles to a minimum number.
- If you do break convention make it obvious what your users need to do.

CONVENTION O'CLOCK

On the grid below, using a good old-fashion pencil (or pen if you are confident!), draw and place these items (including styles) as convention states.

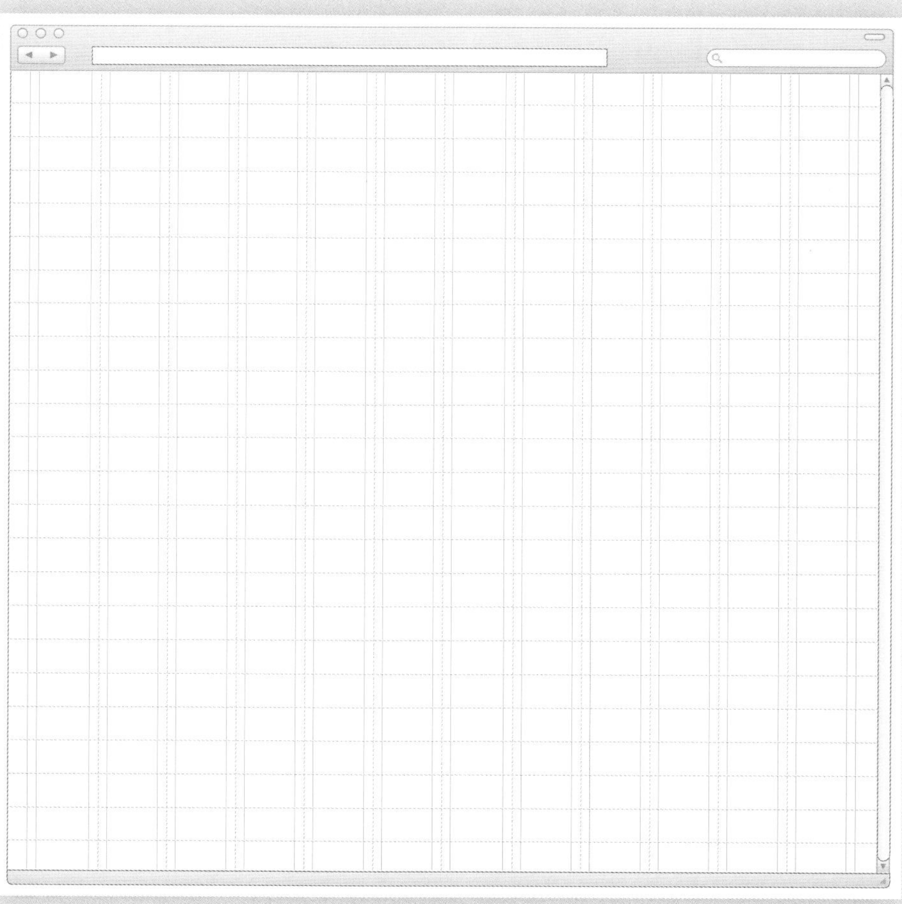

- Logo
- Company slogan
- Search box
- Advanced search box link
- Login and logout
- Horizontal navigation
- Sub-navigation
- Ts&Cs
- Main opening statement
- Associated content
- Promo panel
- Article text and image with contextual link
- Twitter feed
- Social media icons

KNOWLEDGE OF CONTENT

Content is content, right?... Of course, content is content, it wouldn't be content – would it? This chapter goes some way to helping you understand the different types of content, how it can be implemented and other useful content based facts.

I'm going to skip the potential section called 'words'. I think you can guess why, can't you? Well, this isn't a book about how to write and generate content, that's why. But there is a saying in the web community that goes 'content is king'. This means that content is the most important thing on any website, the more of it, the more relevant it is to your users – the better your site is. Search engines like lots of content and spend their days peering over their spectacles reading what's written on your website, like an old school master marking your website and giving it a ranking. If the content is relevant, you will get a good mark. If not, you could end up in search engine detention. :-(

Sad face: this is what is called an emoticon, it is a way of using the standard character set to express an emotion, there are lots of them in use.

A website that only has a small amount of content or hasn't been updated in yonks does not give your potential customers much of a reason to come back. A content strategy is vital for a successful website – as a web designer, you can leave this to the editors.

Content can come into a web page from all manner of sources, not just from sitting there on the page (we call that static content). It can be fed in from other websites, from Twitter, a blog, you name it. That is where the Bento box analogy comes into play again: each one of these content types sits in its own little compartment. Don't forget, when you are styling and marking up these panels, you can do it just the once and decide what other pages you would like it to appear on.

Find out what level of content there will be and how often it will be updated as it will affect how you design the pages and the navigation system.

Contextual links

Contextual links are nothing more than links within context, which is maybe how they got their name, I'm not sure.

Websites like Wikipedia and news websites thrive on contextual links, and are full of words that are links to other web pages or websites within the content of the page – dem be contextual, innit. For the designer the task is to define a style to allow the user to know they are links without making them stand out too much. This is usually achieved by changing the colour slightly or underlining the link. Boy, oh boy, can you get this wrong. If you style your contextual links badly, the site and its readability will be compromised. Yeesh.

SEO Juice: above are two examples of how links within content have been styled.

Contextual links used to be very important for your site's Google ranking, I'm not an SEO expert, so I don't know if that is still the case. Google changes its mind all the time.

Associated content

I've mentioned this kind of content before, but not the myriad of different types it can appear as. The term merely relates to the fact that this content is displayed to the user as something that might be of interest to them. It can be any sort of content: a video, a picture gallery or just another article and can appear anywhere on the site.

E-commerce sites use associated content a lot, showing things like other products you really should buy, or things that you have already looked at but decided not to buy.

Adverts can even be deemed as associated content. A lot of the advertising you will see has been specifically chosen to tempt you, so perhaps when you chose this book, there was an associated content panel offering other books about onions – they don't always get it right!

Associated content tends to sit at the bottom of the page you are looking at or in the right hand column. In terms of their design, they are usually just brief introductions, perhaps a picture and a link to tempt you.

Image galleries and sliders

Like a lot of things on the web, there are conventions and accepted ways of doing things. Image gallery modules are so easy for developers to install that they all end up looking the same and users get used to seeing things 'just so'.

The images for the gallery are uploaded and usually appear in two sizes, a thumbnail for the preview and the full-size image. If you are taking images from a camera, they will have to be downsampled so they are a reasonable size (file size and in physical size) for users to view on a website. One click and the larger images load (into what is called a lightbox) and the user can close the window or click next, etc. There's not a lot of scope there for the designer.

***Stylish:** aside from the fact that (in my opinion) this woman is wearing way too much eye makeup. This image gallery/ slider is nice. If anything, there is too much text.*

But with the dawn of handheld devices and 'hand gesture' navigation, galleries can appear to be more interactive: scroll from the side, animate in and swoop out. All this needs some fancy programming, but all doable.

There are some simple things you can do to make your galleries look great without keeping your developer up all night. They are little more than graphic tricks and in print will not render brilliantly, take a look at knowyouronions.info as per usual for an example gallery.

Briefly, here are a few things to help you make your image gallery look great:

- Use the same size and proportion preview images.
- Add a short description, this helps when you have lots of images illustrating a similar subject.
- Add a one pixel border, this helps if some of your images have a white background. See above for an example and more options.

- Try to equalise the tonal values of the images so that they sit well next to each other. If that is not possible, make the preview images black and white (rollover colour). Clients don't tend to like this solution, but it does looks good.
- Don't ever, ever, mix clip art and illustrations with photography.

Borders

Depending on the background colour of your site, putting a fine border around images really helps, particularly if some of your images are shot on a white background. The key thing is to try to bring some uniformity to a gallery when the user first sees it.

Try a one pixel white line on a coloured background or a one pixel grey line around the image on a white background, that kind of defines them nicely. Or if the background of your site is grey, just leave a grey pixel and then a white one pixel border. The effect is similar, just experiment. It's hard to show this effect in print to be honest, but tiny subtleties on screen make a world of difference to the overall effect...

God is in the details: *this is a detail from the previous page image slider and the style includes grey 1px border, light grey panel, a white 1px border, soft shadow and inner glow.*

Shadows

Shadows are a really easy way to pull an image out of the background for you, the designer. For a developer, it can plunge them into the 'Nightmare of shadows', where they spend all night fighting the evil forces of browser incompatibility. If you look at it this way, unless a shadow is actually part of the image, i.e. already rendered around the edge when it's uploaded, then each shadow has to be created and built to fit around the image. Talk to the developer about it, but don't be surprised, when you are asking for lots of shadows, if they punch you. You can usually get away with it on big carousel images on the home page, for instance. What ever you do, never put them around form fields and generally use sparingly.

Video

Video is much the same as images, but harder to control. If you get the luxury of having edited the video content yourself and controlling what the preview screen looks like, then the world is your graphical oyster. But most of the time, the content is hosted on YouTube or Vimeo and embedded in your page, so the preview image looks the way it looks and that is that.

If the video sits on your own servers it is likely that the developer will use a 'player' to play the content on the screen. You can usually style these, but I strongly suggest you don't start redesigning the play and pause icons because everybody knows what they mean.

Styling video for a web designer is a bit of a pain. Basically: if you host it and edit it, you can do what you like, other than that, you get what you are given – and that's fine, because that's what the user is used to.

Video player: I bought this from a template site, it would take me yonks to draw this up!

Music and sound

Music is similar to video – you will need a player of some sort. These come in all shapes and sizes: some just offer play and stop, others come with graphic equalisers that don't do anything but look amazingly technical. Use sound on a website with caution, extreme caution. If you have an urge to play music on any website that is not specifically about music, don't.

One of the most irritating things is visiting a website and some awful music starts playing and you are then urgently searching around for the off button, whilst the rest of the office looks at you, all of them thinking 'he should be working'. People will accept sound when viewing videos and animations, but not when you are reading the menu for a dodgy Greek restaurant.

There was a 'movement', comfortably quashed I'm happy to say, where so-called 'experts' claimed that users' interaction with buttons should make a sound. What they wanted (and I think they were Scientologists) was that every time you clicked on something, it made a sound. These people failed to realise that A: this is very annoying, B: not something a user has chosen and C: the mouse makes a 'click' sound anyway!

Sound and music should only be used when it is absolutely relevant, or if the user chooses it.

Promo panels

Lots of sites have 'promo panels'. If you want to hire a car, you can bet the home page will feature an offer saying, "Hire this car for only one biscuit a day!" But paying just one biscuit means you can hire it, but you cannot drive it or touch it. In addition to the single charge of a biscuit, you will be charged the equivalent cost of Saturn, plus two million pound excess and even more if you do not bring it back filled up with petrol. (Biscuits in this instance being substituted for your choice of currency.)

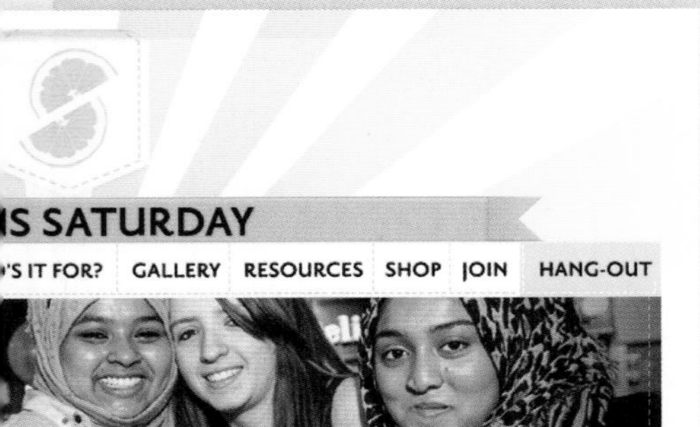

Anyway, promo panels may have to be designed, and if they animate, they become adverts, but that does not matter. They do tend to be graphic rich, so not easily updatable using a CMS. They are something to bear in mind when designing a website and you must accommodate them in your vision.

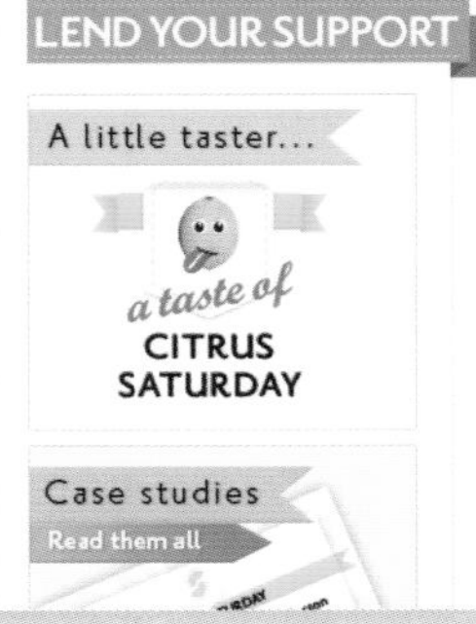

Temptingly clickable: these two promo panels offer a taster day or a case study.

Promo panels usually get updated a lot, so make sure you keep that Photoshop template in good shape so that you can apply a consistent style quickly, whilst still showing the 'offer' in a creative and engaging manner.

Clients will want the promo panel to stand out and say things like, "I want it to really stand out – but not detract from the main function of the site.". As a skilled designer, you kinda know what they mean, or you should. A client's job isn't to make things nice, it's to pay bills.

I have seen promo panels designed to be all 3D and glossy on a website that is essentially 2D. The rest of the site uses flat colour and clean graphics. All of a sudden, someone has designed the promo panel in an entirely different style, not in keeping with the rest of the site, perhaps with the aim of making it 'stand out'. It certainly stands out, but looks uncomfortable. More importantly, it looks like an advert from another site. So watch out for that. A promo panel is part of the site, an advert isn't.

News panels

Having a news panel is popular with clients as it makes their site look up to date and dynamic. And it will if the news gets updated, but more often than not, your lawyer client just won't have the time to update the site because they are too busy charging you eye-watering amounts just for breathing. But that's not the issue; the issue will be firstly designing it, so that the news panel looks right, and helping to keep its integrity once the content editors get their hands on it.

I've mentioned way back that a CMS can restrict the number of words shown in a news panel, but they can also provide an interface for the client to write a news synopsis to a certain character length. This is a very good idea and may not make it into the spec, so check they have thought about it. They can then upload a thumbnail image and link both elements to the full article. Happy days. This is what goes wrong: the image is uploaded and gets distorted to fit the defined size by the developer (the proportions may not be the same), and if they upload an image that is awful and not controlled by the CMS, it breaks the design.

When they write the text too long or too short, the line breaks and text wraps look hideous in news panels. To a certain extent there is not a lot you can do, not unless

Features
The only way is up
Meet the manager of the world's worst football team BBC SPORT

What is a bubble
The joint Nobel winners who fundamentally disagree

Peek-a-boo
The secrets revealed by babies' laughter

Week in pictures
The best pictures from the news this week

Strings attached
How Brazil hopes to reap large rewards from its oil fields

In pictures
A week to record an album in Mali's capital Bamoko

Living lab
How does an urban world continue to put food on the table?
10 things

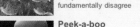

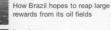

Good news: this example is the best you could ever hope for. Consistent synopsis, decent images and as clear as a bell.

you manage the updates for them. You can provide design guidelines and they will say they will follow them to the letter. Yeah, right.

It's your job to consider the variables (and this applies to all content) and imagine the best and worst case scenarios. Design with these variables in mind and cater for all eventualities. Don't forget to factor in human intervention!

Twitter feeds

Look who's Tweeting: different characters' Tweet feeds are pulled into the site and styled.

Twitter provides its own panel where tweets feed into the page, developers just copy the code, shove the tweeter's name in, slap it into the page code and bing – there it is. Twitter does allow you to customise the panel and change the colour, etc. This external content source and many others can be styled to fit with your site's overall look.

Social media icons

Unless your site is a big social media player, I'd keep those little icons discreet. If you're blogging or writing articles, people are more likely to 'like' things if the icons are at the end of the article or within clicking distance of the thing they are supposed to be liking. Other than that, you can shove them in the footer.

You only have to Google 'social media icons' to see the myriad of different types there are to choose from, from illustrative to glossy in style. Try to choose a set that complements the look of your site, and if there aren't any, design your own. God is in the detail, after all. Don't stray from the accepted icons and start using a giraffe for Twitter, a lot of these icons are recognised because of their colour and their style. There are also a growing number of 'social media' channels that come and go. So, if your site will benefit from somebody 'Pinteresting' something through your Facebook, who found you through LinkedIn and deems it interesting and enlightened to Google+ it, all is well and good. If they do, perhaps you can blog about it?

***Flavours:** there are plenty of styles to fit your site's branding.*

Every website I have designed over the last five years the client has requested I include these in every page. It's sad to see. Take any massive news portal, from CNN to the *Telegraph*, and their articles get single or at really best, double figures in the 'like' factors. Most articles get none. Looks sad to my mind, I wouldn't bother unless you are in a market and have content we really, actually want to like.

***Billy no mates:** it happens to everyone at some point in their lives, you'll get over it.*

Search

Search bars live top right, we know that, right? Most of the time anyway. One little thing that makes a search bar, or any form field for that matter, look nice and save space, is if the 'field names' are actually in the files to begin with.

Like a lot of nice things, it creates extra work for the developers, so speak with them first. You can actually style anything on a web interface. I go into this in more details in the 'Form elements' section on page 59, which doesn't get more anal than that.

The search button should only be one of a few things, where an icon works (I'm an anti-icon extremist), use a magnifying glass icon or the word 'search', or 'go'. I know it's conventional, but stupid things like 'seek', 'check it out', or anything else, just do not work. Save your creative thinking for places where you can justify it and people will understand it, don't change for change's sake.

Advanced searches come in all manner of shapes and sizes, from additional dropdowns, extra fields, check boxes and all that malarkey. As I say, I'll deal with form fields later, but what does make a great advanced search is one that is filtered using tabs to select content types.

Remember to keep these added graphics in style with the rest of the site. If the site uses tabs as part of the navigation system, then mirror the tab style here in the search panel. Make sure you use a similar style for showing which tab is highlighted, if the site uses rounded corners, make sure you add them to all your tabs.

Some searches deliver results 'on the fly', this needs to be carefully considered so that results get displayed in a clear manner, in the smallest space possible.

Search results usually appear in some form of list, with some form of relevance attached to them. Searches can bring back results that cross a wide range of content types, from videos to PDFs. As the designer, you will need to think about how best to show these results and how they have been segmented.

Advanced: *whilst I'm not a huge fan of 3D black Sci-fi style interfaces, an advanced search tabbed interface is clear and saves space.*

The key thing for the user here is speed, as far as you are concerned: the speed and clarity with which the results can be read is important. As far as the developer is concerned, the important thing is getting the relevant results to show. Again, users want relevant results, segmented the way they want them – speed is of the essence.

My suggestion is to make sure you keep the results as lean as possible, such as the title of the document, extraction that is relevant (which is usually with the search terms highlighted) and the links to the main article. Click through, read on, live long and prosper.

Browser form elements

Unless you specify them to be themed, form elements are 'controlled' by the browser. What I mean by that is the way they look depends on what browser you are using. See right. So, just like websites, but more so, form elements render differently, depending on the platform and the browser. You can style them using CSS and actually make them look quite nice (see page 59). These styles are essentially masks that hide what the form looks like, a bit like the Phantom of the Opera (this is a very clever joke but not a very funny one, as Opera is a browser, never mind). The developer will have to spend time making your form elements look good. And trust me, dev will think it is an absolute waste of time. But developers are not designers, and we care about the details, don't we? A really handy template to keep in your bag of tricks is a set of browser elements that you can pull across on to your designs. You may or may not know this, but a check box behaves differently to a radio button. A radio button is either on or off, you can only select one. A check box is used for a list and you can select as many as you like.

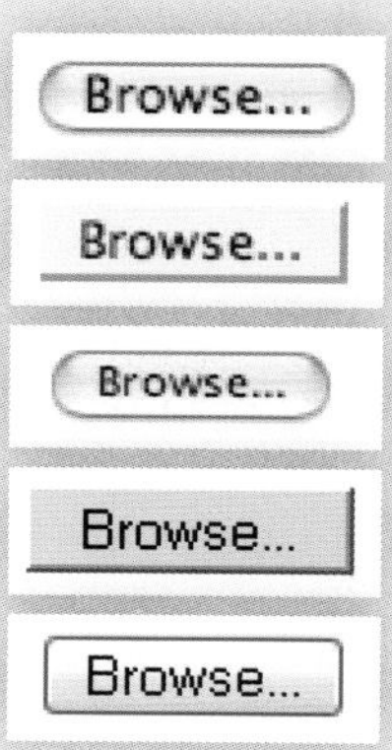

Browse...

Browse...

Browse...

Browse...

Browse...

From top to bottom: *Mac: Safari, Firefox and Opera.*

PC: IE Windows and IE XP.

If you are not going to design your form elements (and that is OK) then keep an up-to-date PSD with them all in, so that you can drag them across to your web designs.

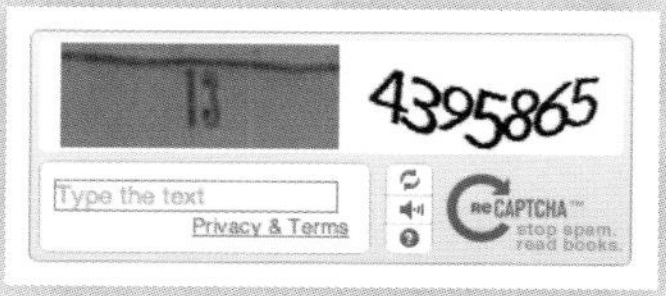

4395865

Type the text

Privacy & Terms

reCAPTCHA™ stop spam. read books.

Gotcha: *you will have come across one of these little blighters. It's called a captcha. They are irritating but do cut down on spam getting through forms.*

Animations

Animations online come in three or four flavours, really:

- **Flash**
- **JavaScript**
- **Gif**
- **HTML 5**

Of course movies can be animations, but in the world of the web, these are the formats that regularly get used.

Flash

Flash, as I've mentioned, is the boss when it comes to animation. I'll tell you all the good stuff first. If you haven't got your head around the difference between vector based and pixel based graphics, you need to. (see page 55). Flash provides a brilliant opportunity to use scalable graphics, vector graphics that never lose quality. The 'price' you pay is twofold: big Flash files have to download into your browsers before you can view them, so you often have to sit there and wait (watching a thing called a 'loading loop') for the file to download. The other thing is Flash, which requires you to download a plugin, which is a bit of software that gets installed in your browser. Like most things, Flash comes in versions and needs updating.

If you are working with a Flash programmer, they can export the files in earlier versions. This can help and avoids exporting files in the most up-to-date version, which users may not have. Of course, new versions give you new functions and the developer will have to tell you if your amazing animation ideas will be compromised by a back save.

This is not a book about Flash design; it's about web design as the title hints at. There are plenty of books out there about Flash and specialist Flash designers who create amazing things. They are heading for history, Flash is like CDs, great when it came out but becoming to be irrelevant.

HTML 5

HTML 5 offers a stack of new functionality, compatibility and opportunities for web design and build. Best of all, it is a 'standard' (as much as it can be). The technology allows designers to use video, audio, vector (side bar) graphics and drag and drop technology, to name but a few. When you have that discussion with your developer about what can be achieved, HTML 5 will give him, and you, the tools to deliver a rich web experience.

JavaScript

JavaScript is one of the resources out there that steps up to the mark and is trying to fulfil some of what Flash can do in terms of animation. It is a scripting language used to extend the functionality in websites. It's executed on the client side, meaning things like validation take place on the user's computer rather than on the server. This makes it nice and fast.

Using JavaScript libraries like jQuery makes it easier to extend the functionality. There are some new JavaScript based applications that can perform some amazing feats, all nicely compatible and quick as you like to download.

Gifs

Gifs: are like flick books: a little thing moves on each page and that's how the animation works.

Animated gifs have been around for years. In Papua New Guinea (in 1843), animated gifs were used to illustrate sacrifices to the Gods. They still are and also to illustrate other commercial aspects of the country. As far as I can tell, when Stone Age man daubed his first wildebeest on the cave wall, he exported it as an animated gif. The technology behind these little files is simple. Tiny files get loaded on top of each other that have changed ever so slightly. Gifs can be transparent, so to speed up the load time, you only need to include the part of the image that changes. Don't expect to be able to animate the Aston Martin sweeping down the hairpin bends of St Tropez, but with practice, and it does take practice, you are able to create some smooth animations in some very small file sizes.

Animated gifs (and Flash animations, for that matter) are used for adverts and file sizes are very important when supplying adverts to other websites. Most websites will give you sizes in pixels and the maximum file size you are allowed to supply. The more frames, colours and transitions in your animation, the more the file size will increase. Until you get used to it, exporting files under what seem impossible and unachievable constrictions, will feel impossible. But over time, you can get there and produce some really quite good stuff. Go online and look at tutorials, chip away at the number of colours and transitions, and eventually you can get that file size down. Believe me, it can be done.

KNOWLEDGE OF TECHNOLOGY

Intranet and Extranet

These terms may sound like they are from The Matrix and out of the normal realms of reality. But they are not. Every day, if you work in a reasonably big company, you will use an Extranet and an Intranet.

If you think about an intranet as an introvert, you are not far off. An intranet is an enclosed environment, perhaps a bit shy, that tends to work for a company. It is the same as the internet, but restricted to a select number of users. Imagine it this this way: Keanu wants to communicate using all the tools that the internet offers, but not to the big wide world, just to the people in his group of desperadoes. That is an intranet. Companies use them to build communities, share information and communicate with people 'in the group'. It is a website or even an internet, for the chosen few.

An extranet is an extension of an intranet and internet, it allows the chosen few (who have login details) to join and become part of the internal offering. For us web designers, this is how it might work.

The in-house team communicate about projects; they discuss how this school may want to talk to another school across the globe. Fine. As an external supplier, rather than the general public, we may have some insight into these discussions and be involved in providing them with, say some strategy. This 'conversation' is not in the public domain, and it is not just internal, it is a middle ground. It's extra.

Crash, bang, wallop

HTML does what is does, but in order to make it do something else, it needs help from JavaScript to Flash plugins. There are bits of software that you have to install, and keep up to date so that when you load a page, the plugin can render the work. Without the plugin installed, it ain't ever going to work.

I would actually bore myself, and definitely you, by going into the complexities of plugins. All that you need to know is, when your ideas get built by the developers, a weird or 'not recognised' plugin will make your site inaccessible. Silverlight springs to mind (look it up).

Some developers will push you to embrace every new technology and get you to install every new plugin or script. To use the example of Sheila in accounts, she is unlikely to care, be bothered, or even know that a plugin may be an issue for her. Be very, very careful crossing the line where your website needs something special to make it work. Sheila is too busy to care.

How it all fits together

What seems like a huge mess of different bits and bobs that make a website, can be consolidated down to a huge mess of bits and bobs. There is no way round it. At the moment, there are too many bits and bobs to make an explanation straightforward. I can't provide you with every different scenario. What I can do, and I am afraid it has to be in a 'Science Teacher' way, is draw some diagrams. These aim to show you how most websites fit together.

Simply put, you register a domain with a domain name registration company. This then 'points' to a server where your website is hosted. A domain name is essentially a mask for an IP address. Every computer (server) has a unique IP address. If your website is database driven, for instance Wordpress or Drupal, then the database is usually hosted there as well.

To complicate things, and why not, the mailserver manages your email. This server need not necessarily be part of the same package.

Static website

www... Domain name

The domain name is registered by an external company and 'points' to the server

Host/server

The server holds all of the HTML files, CSS (controls style), images and graphics

Database driven website

www... Domain name

The domain name is registered by an external company and 'points' to the server

Database

The database holds all of the content and any other data, for instance: subscribers

Host/server

The server holds all of the HTML files, CSS and scripts that chat to the database

CMS driven website

www... Domain name

The domain name is registered by an external company and 'points' to the server

Database ← **CMS interface**

The database holds content, data and the CMS

Host/server

The server holds all of the HTML files, CSS and scripts that chat to the database

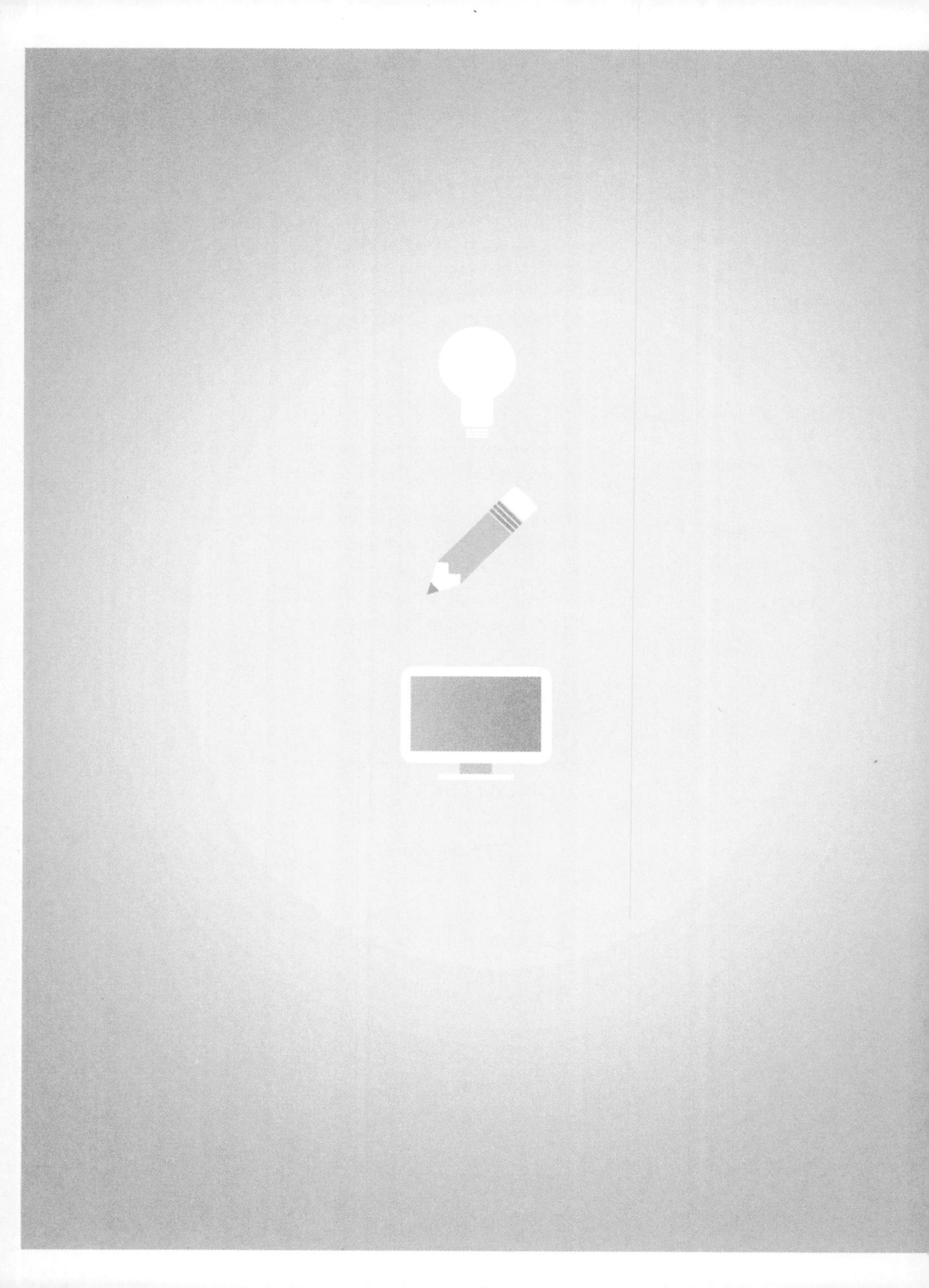

KNOWLEDGE OF THE PROCESS

The brief

Right at the start of this book, we went through a number of scenarios, working on different web projects. We did the 'what if...' thing, remember? Before you can start with any web design project, you need a brief.

Unless you are working with a dedicated team on the client's side (working in-house with the team) the chances are the brief will be scant and only deal with the outline of what the client thinks they want. Thinks. Because more often than not they are not web designers, they won't have thought hard or long enough about what they want. They will assume. An enormous tin of worms opening.

Web design projects suffer more than most because people – that means clients – designers and developers are not clear about what they want to achieve from the start.

I'll say this once (for now), but the more time you spend working on the brief and the scoping document, the better the experience it will be in the end, for everybody.

There will be a resistance, from everybody except the developer, to spend a large amount of time in a project cycle at this stage. Clients want to get up and running as soon as possible and see deep questioning and documentation as stalling. You can tell them a million times it will save time in the long run. It's a bit like watering the garden, if the hose hasn't been wound up properly the last time you used it, then you have to spend ages untangling it as you go along the next time you want to use it (quote Mr J W Eades) and it is a frustrating process. Best to get it right from the start.

In an ideal world, before you even begin to be commissioned, you should have in place:

- *A brief*
- *Architecture or site map*
- *A technical spec and scoping document*
- *Wireframes*
- *Typical user journeys*
- *Target market*
- *Competition*
- *An agreed budget, with contingency*
- *A schedule*

Each element does different things, as you will see. The first thing to knock off is the brief...

Understand your client and their aims

A brief does something that the other documents do not do – it tells you what the client is trying to achieve with the website. Their hopes and dreams, their business needs and what will make them look good in front of their bosses – which doesn't always fit with the other parts of the equation.

With smaller sites, like brochure sites, a brief will be all you get, and to be honest, all you need. For a five page site about your Nan's knitting group, you won't be needing an in-depth scoping document. If you ask for one, she'll look at you over the top of her specs and probably offer you another cup of tea.

Nonetheless, even if it is your Nan, or anybody, you need to speak with them, meet with them and get a written statement of what they want. At best, all of the above.

I mention this five times and it even has its own section on page 63 – that's how important it is.

Assume nothing. This is the mantra for all web design projects.

The brief should contain at the very minimum these things:

- A synopsis of who the organisation/individual is.
- Any brand elements or guidelines.
- What they want the site to do.
- Who the market is, what users they want to attract.
- What the functions of the site will be.

There are other questions that may need to be asked, like how often they need to update the site, whether there is a search engine optimisation plan in place, or at least a need for one. Of course, when you go back and question the brief, which you should always do... what if.

Assume nothing. Nanny could be thinking about bringing her knitting pals into the picture. Maybe getting them to sign up and take knitting commissions. After all, there is a big market for baby clothes, hand knitted by a Granny...

Whether you speak or meet, question things and then write it all down and get it agreed. This is important. Let's say you are asked to design a two-sided flyer for a client and print 1000 copies. There are not many variables in that very scant brief, not many more questions you will need to ask. Maybe, is it full colour? What is the size of the flyer? What weight and finish of the paper would you like? I reckon that covers it. There are not many variables – really.

With web design a whole world of questions present themselves and if you make an assumption (tut-tut), then you could be in for a stack of problems later on. These problems, or misunderstandings, more often than not cause relationship problems, you can end up falling out with your client – you don't want to fall out with your clients. Unhappy people go elsewhere, which means you lose business, which means you lose money. (I'll stop, but I could go on.)

I can't give you every single scenario that you may need to question when figuring out what your client wants. That just isn't possible, but I'll give you one typical situation where what may seem on the outset to be a simple request can turn into quite a complex issue. Here's one.

"We'd like people to be able to sign up to our newsletter"

Right – no problem, below are a few questions that can influence the outcome of such a benign request:

- What fields do the users need to fill in? First name, surname, email, what else?
- Are any of these fields required? 'Required' means the user has to give these details in order to progress.
- What happens to the data after they hit 'sign up'? Does it go to the client as an email, to a database or get written into their email broadcast account?
- What happens to the web page after they have signed up? Does it just say 'thank you' or does it offer them the ability to forward to a friend?
- Does the form need any anti-spam device?
- Does it need to know that someone has already signed up and tell them it's 'OK, you've already signed up, mate'?
- And so on...

I could go on. But as you can see, from what seems on the surface a very simple thing, the functionality has a big bearing on the outcome. 'So what, Drew! I'm a designer, the development team can work this stuff out – right?' Maybe.

But who's going to design the form, make sure the user knows these fields are required, and what the 'thank you' page looks like? Because if you assume it is a given, what you'll get is probably not what you expected and more than likely the client will feel the same. If the user enters an invalid email address (and that checking would have to be part of the scope), then how does that message look? This is all part of your consideration.

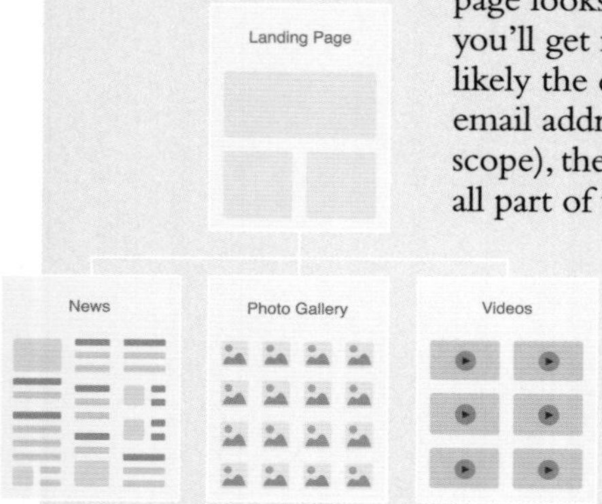

Landing Page

News

Photo Gallery

Videos

To be honest with you, and let's face it, I should be, unless you've borrowed or stolen this book, in which case please read the copyright statement – the scenario above crosses the boundaries of the scoping document. So, I need to move on and get back to the job in hand. I've done my best to detail a web design brief that you can download and send to your clients if needs be. It will not cover everything, but if you have nothing else to hand, then at least it is a start. Oh and guess what, in order to get it, you have to sign up on my website. I tell you what, I do know where my data is going...

You can of course spend time making your architecture documents look great. But I tend to find they distract the client with comments like "does this mean we can only have six videos?"

Architecture

The previous section covered the brief and then went on to touch on scoping a particular bit of functionality, the sign up function. Before we get on to scoping properly, you need to see and understand the sections that will be in the final site and how they fit together. Notice I did not say 'the number of pages'. Most of the time, unless you are designing a very small site, the number of pages is almost irrelevant. Certainly with a content managed site it should be because new pages can get generated at any time with a CMS. The question is, what section do these pages sit under?

Site maps or architecture are the things that define the website's structure and detail structure. We touched on this when talking about navigation. I use the term 'architecture' as opposed to 'site map', because a site map is something you find on a website that helps search engines know what is there for the reading and users sometime resort to clicking on it if all else fails. Architecture covers a bit more than that. Sure, it covers the sections and how they relate to each other, but it also shows inter-connectivity, as much as it can, and perhaps the altered functionality that can occur with different user types.

Wow, 'altered functionality', what does that mean? Well, as an example, if a user has an account with a website, the pages they can see might be different to someone who hasn't got an account yet. Once signed in she may get access to pages that users who have not signed in are unable see.

At a basic level every client you know, even Granny, will know, that the website needs pages and that is the most basic bit of architecture. 'Home', 'About', etc. This is the stuff that makes up your navigation.

In order for you to select the right style of navigation and design accordingly, time needs to be spent detailing the architecture.

There are loads of free and paid for services online that can help you do this, or you can just use something that enables you to draw boxes and lines, s'up to you.

Architecture: this is the site map for knowyouronions. info. The grey line indicates that to get to the resources you must register.

Home **Contact**

About **Books** **Buy** **Courses** **Register** **Resources**

I could have arranged the content like this (below) but chose not to, as the site is a small one and all the pages fit in the horizontal navigation easily.

Home

About **Books** **Courses** **Register** **Contact**

Graphic **Buy** **Resources**

Web

Even with the biggest site in the world, the architecture process shouldn't be such a big deal, really, although the way some of my clients react you would think we were writing the Magna Carta. It is important to go through the process. Without doing it, I don't think you can begin to design, unless you are mad.

Architecture defines the structure of the site. It does not show every single page and it does not show every single link. If it did, the whole thing would have so many lines all over it that even a spider would find it confusing.

Do you see how clear it all is? Sometimes it does need explaining, sometimes, clients will say 'OK', but I need them to be able to see 'Contact', when they are in the 'My account' section. That's OK, they will. I'm going to stick my neck out here, big time, and put together the architecture for a massive UK (and, of course, global) site: Amazon. The example to the right does not detail every single product page. How could it? For starters, the architecture probably changes every day, but it does go some way to show how the site and its content is organised so that users can find what they want. Fingers crossed, and sorry Amazon if I get it a bit wrong.

For such a massive site like Amazon, it is amazing how a simple architecture diagram can distill down the huge structure into an understandable arrangement.

No matter the size of your site, get this bit done, discuss it with your client, talk about how it might expand in time. For instance if they add a whole new section, how will that fit into the architecture? After all, Amazon started by just selling books... now look at them, they don't even pay tax!

Get it agreed and signed off. With the architecture document and the brief, you are a good way down the road to knowing what on earth you need to design.

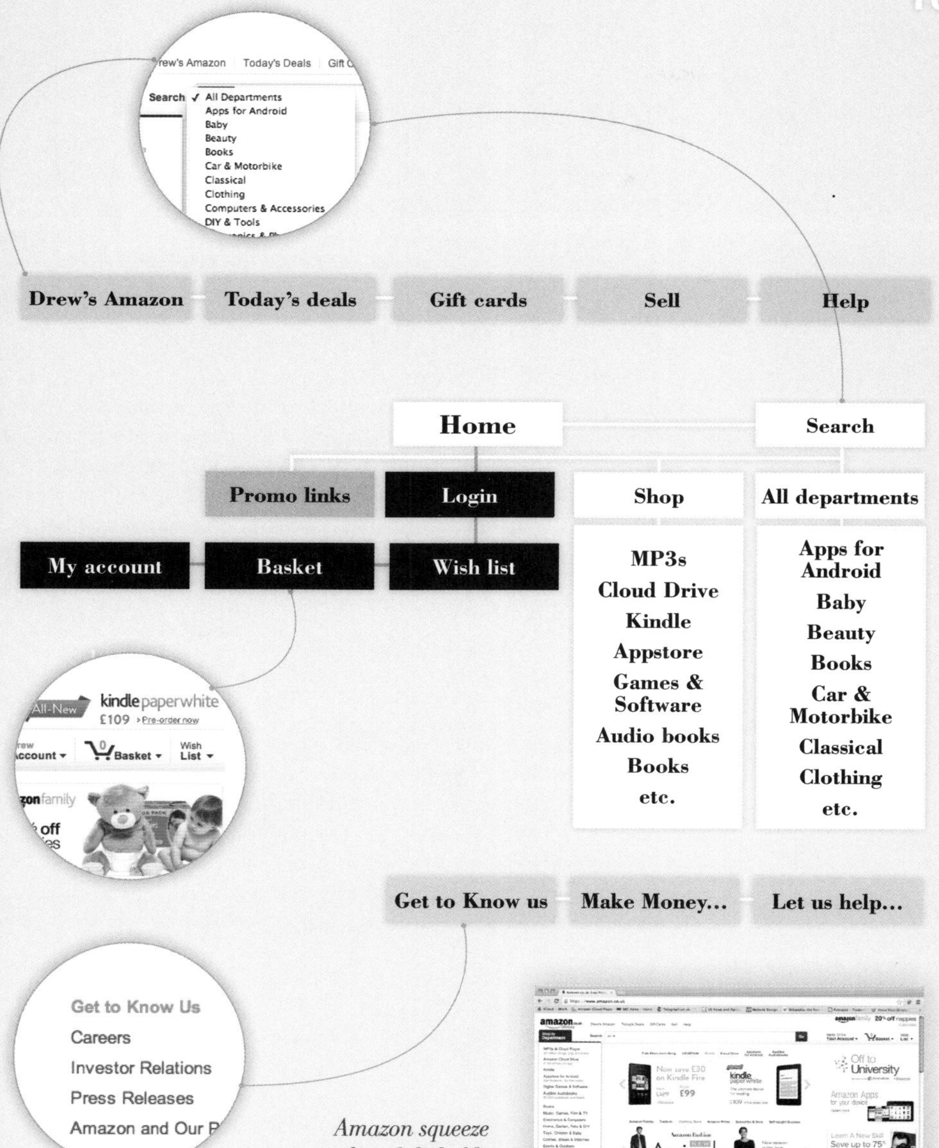

Amazon squeeze a lot of clickable content on their home page.

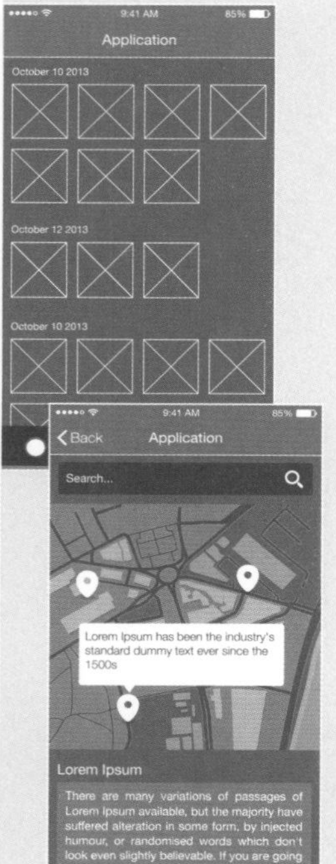

Wireframes don't have to be ugly: the one above is for a mobile app.

Wireframes

Wireframes are not always necessary, certainly not on smaller sites with a low level of functionality. They do the job that architecture can't and scoping goes on to explain in detail. Let me explain.

A wireframe details what appears on key web pages in terms of the elements, and that includes the navigation, content types and a bit of functionality. They do not dictate design. I'll come to that in a bit.

Wireframes, like their name suggests, are ugly things, put together using wireframe applications with no regard for aesthetics or usability. And that is just how you need them. What they do is illustrate, sometimes page by page, what will appear on the specific page. This cannot be achieved in the architecture document, because that document is too high level, it isn't detailed enough. Wireframes drill down to a page level and show what the designer will need to address, element by element. That does not mean that a wireframe needs to be produced for every single page on any given website, but all of the key pages.

Wireframing is a stage needed for relatively large sites where key pages and sections need to be detailed so that clients and the rest of the digital team (including you) can get their heads round what needs to be there on a specific page and what might happen. Let's use the gentleman's outfitter as an example. We'll assume that we have the brief. For good measure, I'll include what I think the architecture should look like:

Home

- **Shop**
  - **Formal**
  - **City**
  - **Country**
  - **Casual**
- **Search**
  - **Department**
  - **Item**
    - **Neck tie**
    - **Bow tie**
- **Etiquette**
  - **Resources**
- **Register**
- **Contact**
  - **Returns**

Note: I have not icluded the footer in this architecture diagram.

Now, let's take an example page, the 'Neck tie' page – what needs to be there? Well, we want to show the range of ties, that's for sure. What else? Well, we might want to show all manner of things and the things we might want to show should be detailed in the wireframe.

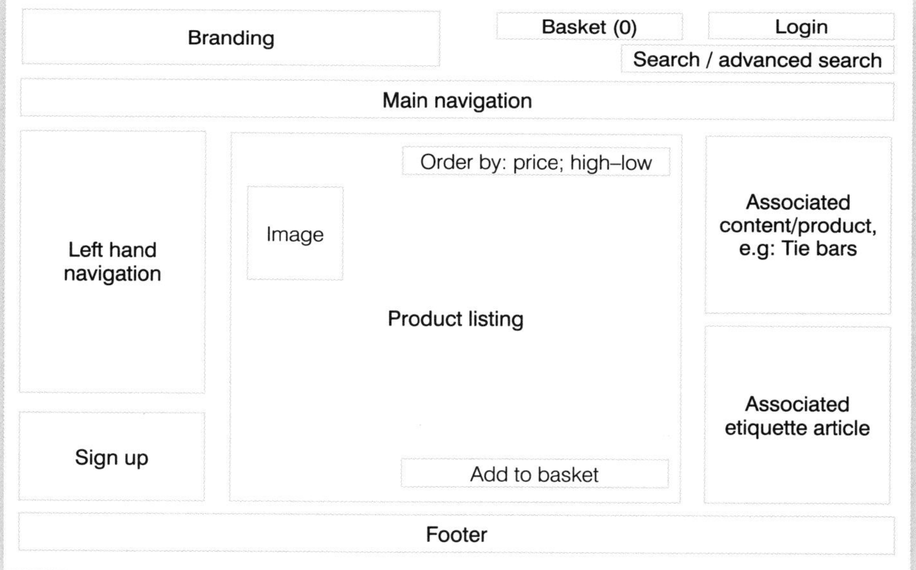

Some of your big clients will go through this process for you, which doesn't mean you can't make suggestions when you see the wireframes – you should. Some smaller scoping or web design projects don't really need wireframing. It all depends on the project.

Wired: you should be able to see from the wireframe above, all the elements that will feature on the 'Neck tie' page. The wireframe is a glorified contents page that makes things super clear.

Wireframing, perhaps more than a lot of things, focuses the mind. All of a sudden, here it is, in black and white, in big ugly boxes – all the things they want and need their web pages to do and include. It will focus your mind, it will focus the client's mind and help focus the developer's mind. (Tip: focusing everybody's mind, agreeing scope and responsibilities, and getting sign off at milestone stages are vital to achieve a smooth-running web project.)

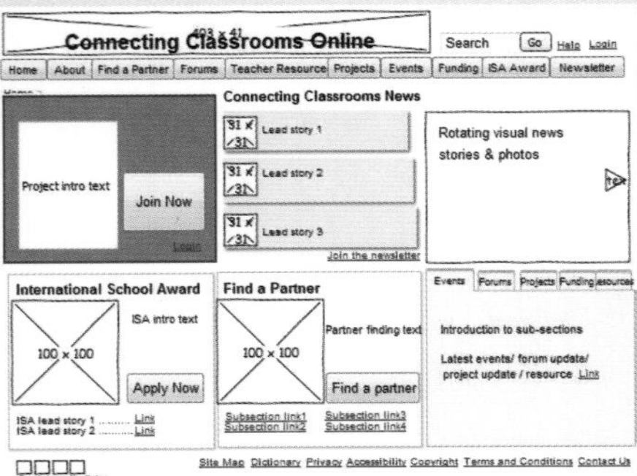

If you are in a position to get these babies signed off, happy days. However, whether you do the wireframing, or the UI expert does, what needs to be clear in everybody's mind is this – the final design may not follow the exact same structure shown on the wireframes themselves. People who put wireframes together will plonk a certain piece of functionality on the page, anywhere on a page. That does not mean it is the right place, nor that it has the right weight or importance on that page. That is down to you, my friend. The person doing the wireframe might stuff the search box bottom right, but as excellent designers, we know that sticking it there breaks convention and probably isn't the best place for it. Capiche?

Above: this is the wireframe for the site below.

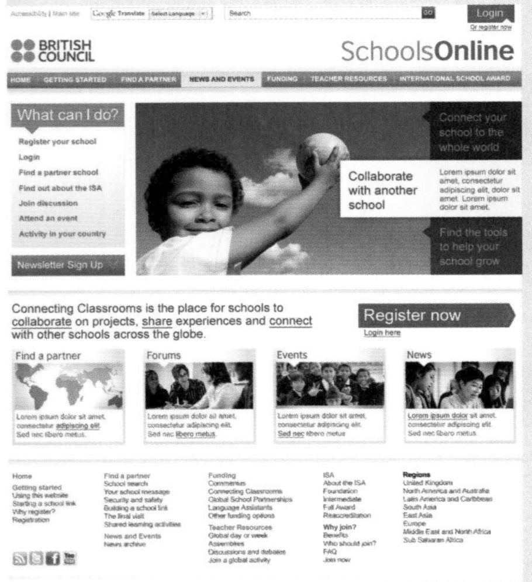

This can often result in a bit of a battle between you and 'Captain Wireframe'. You are well within your rights to fight it using special 'Design Man' powers of persuasion. It will depend on how experienced you are and how experienced the person who did the wireframes, is as to who knows what is best. But like all design projects, collaboration with the experts in their fields will deliver the finest results. Work together, discuss things, listen to opinion and learn from the experts. Anyway, the long and short of it is this, the wireframes are a far more detailed description and definition of the site on the page. When you need to detail what the site does and what happens when a user does something, then you need a scoping document.

Scoping

Yesh, I promised you this book was all about design and here I am talking about scoping. Bear with me. If you are an architect or a product designer, you do not need to be a builder or a manufacturer – right? But you do need to understand that RSJs do one thing and aluminium extrusions do another. This, of course, has nothing to do with scoping or what is often called the 'technical specification'.

These documents are primarily meant for the development team. They detail what happens in terms of database structures, functionality, code, compliance, square route and archipelago to name but a few. Remember the 'sign up' to a newsletter example I used? The answers to the questions I raised in the form example? The answers to these questions, and all relating to the functionality of the website, should be in the scoping document.

On the biggest sites the technical scoping is, to be frank, the most important thing. As a designer, you'll work with and really understand the functionality of the site. The way things work, how the thing interacts and what happens after the event, has a massive effect on the budget and the technology used.

I'm not asking you to understand the technology; if you did, you would be a developer. But it is important to understand the importance of this document and how it fits in the process. It does not matter how good the brief is, how clear your architecture is and how ugly your wireframes are. If the developers don't know how to build the thing or what is expected of them, then the whole thing is kaput.

It is difficult to give you an example of a scoping document as they vary hugely depending on the website. No matter what, this bit of the process does need to be done. The client will need to be involved, you should be involved, the dev team must be included, as they are the boys and girls who can advise the best way to make it all work.

Do your best to be in the meeting, even if you have no idea (at first) what is going on. As you sit there, they may say things that may sound alien, perhaps they sound like they are speaking Klingon, but go anyway. Over time, you will learn to understand Klingon, even if you do not understand their culture.

Example Q & A

Q 1.0: What path will users take to arrive at the application form?

A: They will click on a link on the college's own website and arrive at an application page, branded with the college logo and begin the registration process.

OR

A: They will click on a link on the college's own website and arrive at an application page branded to look like the funder's US website and select from a dropdown:

The college closest to the applicant

or

The region the college is in and is closest to the applicant

And/or

There will be a dropdown and a map indicating the regions available in the US

and so on...

I've been lashed by a reviewer for not going into enough detail about things. How can I? Why should I? This book sets out its stall very clearly, read it and know what's what. If you want to specialise or have a deeper understanding of a particular issue, there are books that deal with each and every subject in this book individually – with the exception, of course, of the secrets I've learnt and shared with you.

I hope I don't have to point out that these terms are not related to website code. However, Ubuntu, Magneto and Ruby on the Rails are and they sound equally mad!

I still feel the same way now when I'm in these meetings. I suspect I will always feel this way because just when you think you've got your head round what is happening technology changes and everybody is speaking Nimbari, Klingon is no longer compatible with Urdu, or whatever.

I don't know your situation, but people are people and most of them like coffee and cake or beer or whatever. A chat outside the meeting room with other team members can help you to get an idea of what is going on and help you to understand how your design work needs to fit with what they are doing. Ask questions, learn – don't be afraid to ask.

Brand understanding

The next step as far as you, the designer, is concerned, is brand understanding. Again, we touched on this in our early project examples. This is down to you and is an important stage in the process. Like the developer needs to know how the thing should work, the designer should know how to make sure the thing is on brand.

With luck and a south-easterly wind, you will have a brief. But most likely that will not be enough to help you give the client what they need. This is the stage when you have to really look at what the client wants to achieve with the website and mould their desires into something that builds their brand, does the job and blows a user's mind.

How can I tell you how best to achieve this? How many brands are there in the world and how do they differ, what makes them unique? My life, I can't. What I can do is ask you, the designer, in this stage to take some time, look really hard at what is out there, be sensible, practical and, above all, be creative.

You are clearly a highly intelligent person because you have bought this book and bothered to read it. Apply intelligence to the brand application and be creative. Look at the style of the graphics, the tone of communication and the way your client communicates with their market within their brand.

If you are working for a big brand, some of this will be dictated to you. If you are working on their corporate site, then you really need to make sure your designs fit with their corporate feel. To some extent, if you have been commissioned to design a micro-site or something a bit special then you can let your hair down a bit. But only a bit. And only if you understand the brand in its entirety.

If you are in a situation where you are presenting to a client and they turn around and say, "You don't really understand our brand", then you should be ashamed of yourself. I am not saying that you should not push the boundaries. You definitely should. The what if process is all about that, after all. What I am saying is, make sure no matter what barriers you push, the site still fits with the brand.

Branding understanding: *unless of course they don't understand their brand either!*

There are a number of things, detail really, that help make sure you have at least some of it right. These include:

- Font use.
- Colour pallet.
- 3D or 2D graphics, to a certain extent.
- Use of images, be it photography or illustration.
- Tone of voice, how the brand speaks about itself.
- And, of course, style.

Once you have your head around these issues and the brand values ('The principles of applying brand' goes into some of the finer points), you can start to develop concepts. Yippee, design at last!

Concepts

We've been through the whole 'use a pencil thing', right? Hopefully you have got to a place where you have developed your designs ready to show the client. You have got a design showing exactly what they have asked for, something a little more interesting and something amazing, right?

My spilling, typing and grammor is awful – some of you will have noticed that.

Go back and read the brief. Read it again. Don't just go "Yer, that's right.". Is it really? Look at your concepts, check the architecture is right, check your spelling. If a client is looking at your groundbreaking design, they will get distracted if you have spelt something wrong. In fact, that is all that they will see. They focus on little errors and just can't see the big picture, so get those little details right.

Park the designs for a day or two, don't look at them. Come back to them with fresh eyes. If like me, your eyes are jaded, use somebody else's; ask them to look at your design and give feedback. Don't give them any pointers as that will steer their minds to giving you the answers you want, just let them look at your work without influence. We have somebody in our team called 'client head'. (Side bar, this is not her real name, her real name is Baroness Client-head.) She just thinks like a client, not a designer. Occasionally, she pipes up something that has a devastating effect on the designs, but nearly always she is right, because she thinks like a client and a user. Don't go to the table and present with something you are unhappy with, but do make sure you present something relevant for the users. If you don't, you have let yourself down.

Make sure that you are in a position to explain every single thing that you have done and justify your decisions. I had a client the other day, who had briefed me on a design project and said, "I want you to redesign the interface for this website, I mean, who on earth chooses a dull grey background for a website?" Off I went and designed her a website with a nice white background. However, my middle solution used a light grey background. She liked the design, but questioned me why I had done this. After all, I had apparently ignored one of the things she had specifically pointed out in the original design that she did not like!

My reason was this: most of the site content was panel based, so I could put a border around the panels to make them stand out from the background but that would look messy and fussy. What we needed was to gently push the content forward, so each panel was a white background on a very, very pale grey. It was subtle and made the content stand proud just enough. I explained it to her and she loved the grey.

Presentation

I think the best way to present website concepts is to upload them to a server as jpegs, but you have to do a few things first, otherwise they can look rubbish. You can always email them as attachments, which is fine, but it means they see them out of context and, of course, being a static jpeg it can't show what happens when you click on something. You could send loads of different jpegs, showing all the different states of the page, like rollovers and dropdowns, but that is tedious for everyone.

I suggest that you compress your jpegs, so that they are still high quality, and embed them in an HTML file. If the site is to be centred, for instance, centre the HTML and the graphic inside. If the background colour is grey or whatever, colour the HTML file background the same. It takes a tiny bit of effort, but makes a big difference.

If you have no idea how to do this, that's OK as well. If you can handle dumping a jpeg into an HTML page and uploading it, then I've got a few on the website you can use. I'd suggest changing the page tiles to match the concept. I'd also suggest that you copy and paste the URLs into an email so that at the end of the presentation you can email the client the links and they can share them.

For the reasons stated above, you cannot show in a static visual how the page will interact, so it is a very good idea to be in front of your client when you show them your designs and explain what is what.

But what to show? Clients like to see home page designs. Of course they do, this page will be the most important on the whole site. As I have said earlier, it may not be the first you choose to design, as a home page is a culmination of the content of the whole website. But, nonetheless, you probably need to show it. Also, show a typical 'static' page, like 'About'. It's boring, but will show that you have applied your design to all aspects of the site and can make anything look good. Lastly, select a key function page. If it is an e-commerce site, then show a page that displays the product and how you can buy it. And that's it. Any more at this stage and you run the risk of putting shed loads of work into something they may not like.

We go to the presentation with three ideas – what they asked for, what they could have and something that will blow their mind. So, that's three designs and three pages each. That's a lot of work and a lot for them to take in.

Leave it with them. Ask them to correlate the responses and offer to speak with them at any time to discuss the designs. Remember this, when they commission you, they will have something in their mind. They will have imagined what they think they have briefed you to do. You can be 100 per cent sure that what you have shown them will not be what they are expecting. So, it will take time and an explanation.

Design development

With a fair wind, a four-leaf clover and your mojo working, you will have presented something that excites the client – if you're lucky, or if you have done your job properly – they want to move forward with it.

Listen to what they have to say and give them a call to discuss what they want and try to find out why they want the changes they want. I say this because clients will try to manipulate and change the design to resolve an issue they may have in their heads. What you should be doing is trying to understand what the issue is and bring a solution about. This is a very important thing to understand.

If you don't do this, you can get in a situation where a client will chip away at a concept, instructing you to do this and that, in the hope that you will give them what they want, or solve that nagging issue that you have not defined.

The extreme of this is when a client just won't listen and would rather design the website themselves, if only they knew how to use Photoshop and Dreamweaver. I've known this to happen and it never ends with a good result that the client is happy with. Sometimes you just have to think about the money.

OK, so you have rung your client, talked through the changes, listened to what they have to say, questioned things and assumed nothing.

Now go about resolving those issues and stick to that mission like a laser beam. Fix those issues. Apply the solution or, if there is more than one solution to the client's chosen route and problem, show them both. Of course, if they don't like anything you presented, then go back, find out why you were so far off the mark and start again.

Apply the solution to the two or three pages and get them to review again. This process can go through a number of iterations. Once you have it right, get the client to agree these pages. This is important, because now you have to tackle all the other pages in Photoshop and that takes time. If the client is not 100 per cent happy with, say, the text styles it will take you yonks in Photoshop to edit it all. Interestingly enough, it wouldn't take a developer very long to change the text styles, as he or she will just edit those little CSS files, but it will take you a long time in Photoshop.

So get it agreed and then tackle the rest of the work. These little milestones in projects are important and it is a really good idea to detail these in the schedule. I've put a process and a very, very loose schedule online for you guys. Every project is different and, of course, every team and every designer works differently, but take a look, make up your own mind, edit as necessary: knowyouronions.info.

Sign off ready for build

At this stage, you should have applied your design to all the key pages on the site, from the home page to the static pages to the highly interactive ones. You need to make sure you have covered everything. If your site is going to have a forum, make sure you have spoken to the dev team and addressed the styles that you can change. This applies to anything that will get integrated into the site, so check the scoping document and check you have covered every content type.

Don't forget the elements page. It is difficult to lash a developer because the style for a bulleted list is inconsistent if you haven't provided the styles, marked up properly.

Developers don't always get what the elements page does. Actually, lots of people don't explain it and, my gosh, it saves work when the developer comes to theming and styling the site-wide elements.

Present your suite of designs to the client, go through the development stage, take on board what they have to say, and do all that is necessary to get sign off. Written sign off. This is a big milestone. Get it right here and build will be speedy, you and the developer will have the 'tools' to make sure the final code matches your vision and the client's aims.

The important issue here is this, what may seem a small change later could cost hours of development work. This work is usually extra, I mean, it can be charged extra. While that is acceptable in your mind, it can be hard to help a client understand why it costs so much.

For example, let's say you decided back in the day to use graphics instead of live text for your headlines. That's all cool if they don't change too often and there are only a few headlines on the website. But now, the client decides Rockwell would look way better if it was Franklin Gothic, or even a web safe font like Georgia. In the Franklin Gothic example, you will have to go back and change the font on your headlines to Franklin Gothic and resupply the graphics to the developer. In the second instance, what really should happen is the developer needs to recode the headlines to be live text in Georgia. Yikes! Such a small change, but a reasonable amount of work. Chargeable work. Explain that sign off before this stage means, if you want to change things later, it is more work.

Look at it from the client's point of view. They have all these fonts and lots more on their machines, which means they can open a program like Word and just change the font. Badda bing. So why can't you just do the same? Why are you charging extra for this, you robber? Don't assume they know what is involved.

Perhaps I should have called this book, 'Don't assume you even know what an onion is'. It has a certain Mafioso feel about it, don't you think? "Yo Mikey, don't assume, you get hurt that way."

So, get it right, get it signed off. Then get it ready for build.

SIGN-OFF:

Written sign-off helps focus the client's mind and clarifies whose responsibility it is to check the content and functionality. It's not unusual for there to be a number of phases, milestones or approval rounds during a website development project. They go something like this:

I confirm that I (insert the client) have reviewed and approved the design and development of the (insert project name) website as designed by (your company) and presented to me on (insert date).

I accept and acknowledge that any further revisions or new work to the approved website may incur additional charges. Please proceed to deploy.

Signed

Date

Getting it ready for build

It's worth copying in the dev team to the final set of visuals. They usually ignore them, but hey, we are a team, right?

Some developers will just take your PSDs and hack them about and build it. Unless you are working on a really small site, this should ring alarm bells. What does happen in my experience is if the site becomes one enormous graphic, neither editable, viewable nor another-able.

Mark it up: *as you can see below, my team have marked up the elements of the website in pixels to help the developers build the site and at least have a hope in hell of it looking something like the original designs.*

This next bit will be either a pain in the Rupert or something that you see as the final polish to a piece of work. It will depend on what kind of person you are. If you stack your shoes in the bottom of your wardrobe by colour, season and style, then you'll love this. If you live in a skip and drink neat spirits because you can't be bothered to go to the corner shop to buy a mixer, which is literally on the corner (not my typical readership), then you'll hate this.

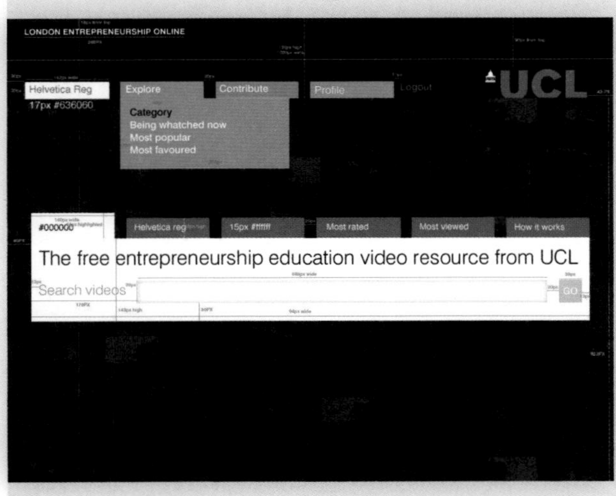

LONDON ENTREPRENEURSHIP ONLINE
Helvetica Reg
17px #636060
Explore
Contribute
Profile
Logout
UCL
Category
Being whatched now
Most popular
Most favoured
#000000
Helvetica reg
15px #ffffff
Most rated
Most viewed
How it works
The free entrepreneurship education video resource from UCL
Search videos
GO

Now you need to mark up your designs, in pixels, on a layer or in a folder containing layers, called 'mark up'.

If your pages are not pixel perfect, it will show now. If you slipped off the 960 grid, or your graphic is one pixel too wide, if you don't get it right now, more than likely, it will get built like that. Don't assume the developer will say to themselves "Oh my, Billy is a pixel out on this graphic, so it's wider than the box, what should I do?" because they won't give a moment's thought to it. They'll be thinking about implementing this new, amazing script that means they're the 'dev master' and all other developers will be in awe of their scripting skills.

See page 61 for more on marking up your PSDs.

Mark it up in pixels, be precise, leave nothing to chance.

Build and testing

At this point in the process, you can kick back, chill, lay down some chords and shoot the breeze. Because the dev team have to now take what you, in your fancy designer ways, have dreamed up, and make the thing a reality. Ain't dat the truth?

Yes, it is the truth. Like a print job, it is now time to hand over the design and let the guys and gals in the development team make it happen. However, with most things print, it just happens. They take your artwork and a few days later, this lovely smelling, tactile thing arrives on your desk – a nice printed job.

With web design and build, you can still shoot the breeze, but you need to be around. First of all, if you can do this without irritating the arse of the developers, ask them to look at some test links, or even look over their shoulder, as things progress. What you are likely to see is your design all over the place, with those carefully crafted content types strewn across the Bento box, looking like somebody has come in and robbed the place. This is because your dev team are working through the process and the last thing on their minds is how it looks and where it sits on the page. What matters to them is that it is there and it works.

I think it is important to see this process; it gives you an understanding of how things get done. Best to keep schtum and let it happen, just be on hand if they have questions or need a graphic sorting.

Developers will work locally, i.e. on their own machines where they mirror what it would be like when the site is live. When they get to a stage where they need to upload to a server to test to see if something works, they will provide you with a test link. Unless, as a designer, you are really experienced and understand the development process, it's best to wait until you get a link through from the developer, with what *they* think is a test link.

I italicised 'they' because 99 per cent of the time the work isn't right. And that is OK. It is part of the process and you should see it that way. Developers are not like printers, there are too many variables in development work to get it tested and right first time – most of the time. You can't push a button that says 'build' and out it pops. Don't expect it and don't allow your clients to expect it either.

The first step is to test the work yourself, unless you have a huge team behind you – then someone else may have the task of doing the testing for you. Either way, the first round of testing is a basic test – does it look OK (only OK) and does it work? Probably not. You have to take this stage for what it is, an early test and this is not the time to deal with the nitty gritty of the design and functionality implementation.

I've worked with so many developers, from the Eastern European freelancer, the in-house developer, to some of the biggest and most respected development companies in the world. Most, if not all, will perform a cursory test on their work. Nearly always it does not work as it should.

As a designer, and as a client, really – you need to make a shift in expectations. What you may think is that all code should be validated and correct, platform tested and working in all environments, including the Tiangong space station. But life just isn't like that. When you get the first test link, just expect to have to give feedback on a number of issues, think of it as a prototype, as that is what it is.

Project managers make the mistake of promising client code ready to go on first test link. It's so rare when that happens, if ever, PMs get pressured by clients to get it done quickly and fire off a link. The client then goes online and the thing does not work. If you are a PM, even if you think you know this, please, take some responsibility and get the dev team and the designers to go through and check it first.

If, my mighty designer, you do not have this team behind you, then test yourself.

At this point (in some instances) you will need to become schizophrenic, or even better, assume multiple personalities, because you will have to test as yourself, the designer, as the client and, worst of all, the user.

Quality check

You will need to go through a top level check way before the client sees the test link. Do it and feedback what needs to be fixed in a considered and organised way. Use a bug tracking system (look it up) or any system that will correlate your comments. Do not fire back comments and amends in hundreds of emails. The developer, like anybody, will find this hard to manage and, without a doubt, miss things. Collect everything up and send over a set of comments and amends that are well documented and explained. This document will be your checklist so that you can tick off each issue and make sure everything is tickety-boo.

Not OK: this is a very typical render problem that needed to be fixed, the text panel is deeper than the sign up bar and the cream background does not fill the whole cell.

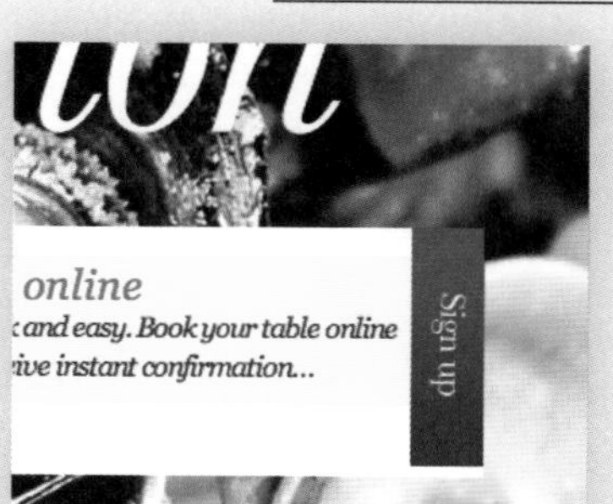

I'll assume here that you have worked closely with your dev team and been through the first, top level test.

If you are in a good place, and that place means you have time to check the work, and somebody else has been tasked with checking the code and functionality so that the site performs as the client wants it to, then the last thing to consider is how a user might experience the site.

What usually happens, for some unknown reason, is the deadline is so short that the client wants it now! And before you know it, they are looking and clicking on things that aren't quite ready, and you know what happens then – they get annoyed because it's not perfect.

In a quality check, as a designer, you aim to make sure the web pages render as you intended them to in a reasonable amount of browsers, platforms and devices. This should be outlined in the technical spec or scoping document, so that the developer knows what level of platform compatibility they need to adhere to. To make everything absolutely pixel perfect will cost.

And so, from our three personalities we need to test, record and feedback, and test again, in terms of our quality check. After all, three heads are better than one. Here we go.

Test as the designer

This is easy. You know from your visuals how you would like the website to look. You can bet your bottom dollar that the developer will be working on a PC and you will be working on a Mac. So they will build it to make it look as close as they can to your visuals on a PC. Load that into a Mac browser and it will never look the same. So you have to choose, compromise and aim for the best possible result. Sad to say that the world is still dominated by machines that all treat and render things differently: until that changes – accept it. PCs rule the roost, so best to get it looking right for the majority.

So, before you start throwing your weight around, you need to look at your new shiny website on a few PC browsers. If needs be, get some screen snapshots done so you can compare the render on different platforms.

There is a phrase called 'transform gracefully' which means that, although the site will never look the same on different computers and platforms, the overall effect will reflect what the original vision was. Transform gracefully (what a great, elegant phrase, like ballroom dancing) means to take the essence of your vision and make it work as beautifully as it can in any given environment.

Degrade gracefully and graceful degradation mean the same thing, but I don't like the sound of them as much.

So take a view, look at how things render and aim for the best reasonable result. You can use online tools that help the developer to see what other users see in their different browsers and the myriad of platforms. Developers can include bits of code that try to compensate for different browsers. Different browser versions can be very stroppy and refuse to accommodate and display your content, as they want to do things their way. Essentially what happens is the code says to these awkward types, "oh, you have this browser and because you had this really bad experience as a teenager, we need to display things a bit different so that you don't get upset?"

Again, there are lots of 'EMO' type browsers and platforms out there with weird render attitudes – but they are out there – and the people who use them may want to look at your site. Try not to leave anyone out, no matter how niche they might be.

Take a view, work with the developer, get the best you can. Remember that this world (the online world) isn't like print where everything is fixed and when you hold it in your hand, it looks and feels the same for you as it does for the next man.

Content upload

At some point, the content for the website you have designed and built has to be uploaded or put into the pages. In a tiddily website, or a static site, the words and pictures are put in as the website gets built. On bigger sites, the content and the links are entered using the CMS, after the site framework has been built. This can take a long time and tends to be an ongoing process, sometimes alongside the development and build process.

No clue: a classic example of a client sourced image – meaningless.

As a designer, you will want to make sure that your graphics and images are of fine quality, beautifully cropped and compressed to a file size for fast download. Which means as small in file size as it can be without looking shockingly awful. You will want to avoid clients uploading meaningless images that they have got from an image library on the internet at all costs. Clients like doing this because they can be 'creative', bless 'em.

Somebody needs to upload content into the new website, either from the existing website or new content that is generated for purpose.

And, of course, what seems a straightforward activity in the web design process becomes complex, only because there are so many different scenarios.

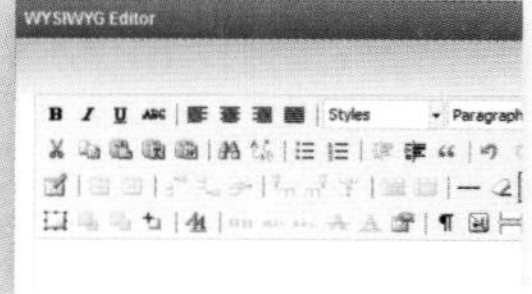

If you are building a CMS website, then of course you can give the client access and allow them to upload the content themselves. They will need to understand how the system works and what is expected of them. Most CMS these days come with WYSIWYG interface that allows the users to style text, add links and images, etc. As I've said before, there are lots of different CMS out there and, for me, Drupal wins hands down.

WTF?: no, not WTF, but What You See Is What You Get... like the interface above.

The content editors are either going to be using old content (probably from a previous version of a website) and reviewing it, or new content altogether. This is the time for them to look at their SEO strategy and, as they edit the text, they can enter in the page titles, meta descriptions, etc.

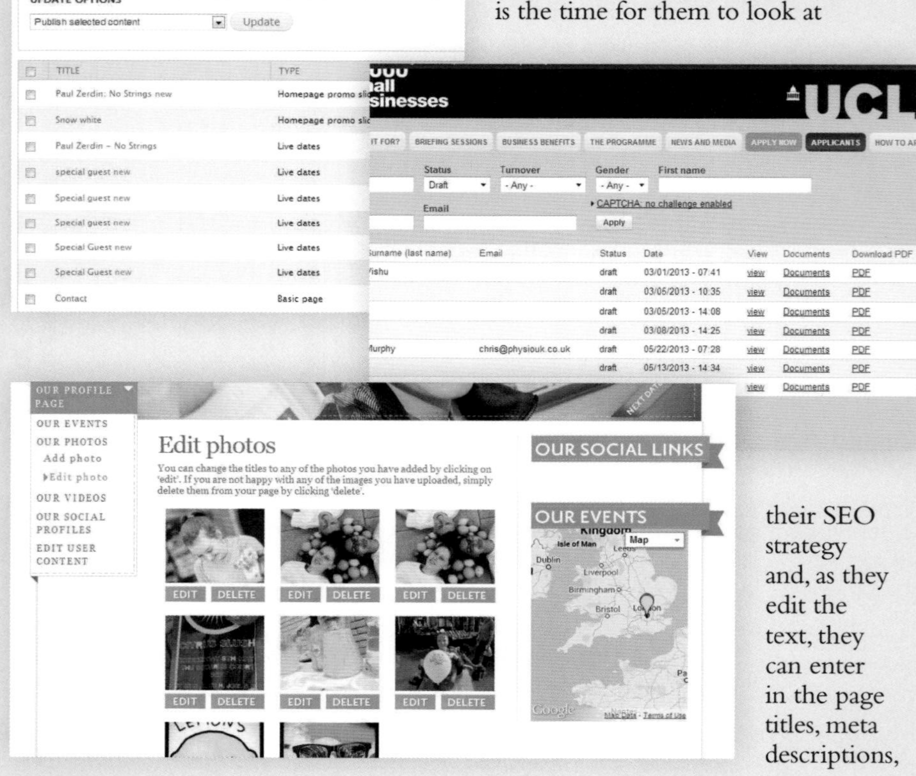

Top to bottom: these are all snapshots of the Drupal admin area in the CMS, The top is not styled, the other two show the levels of styling that can be achieved.

If the team looking after the website is big enough, often content editors will 'queue' third work for the big old webmaster to check and approve before making live. Who gets access to what pages and sections in the site is controlled by the permissions set by the 'admin users'. Some content editors will only have access to the section they are sponsored for. The styles for the text, etc., are set in the system, so that they don't (or shouldn't) mess about with the way it looks.

Functional testing

Someone now needs to go through the whole website and test that the thing works. Ideally, the developer should do this and present a fully functioning site – this will never happen, I'm afraid. Developers expect someone else to test functionality, so do designers, and clients don't like doing it either. At the beginning of the project it should be clear who is responsible for the testing and to what degree. It should be clearly stated who will sign off on the functionality, and when it is tested.

From a client's perspective, they will say, "Why should I do it, I'm paying the agency to build something that works. If I have to test everything, I'm doing their job for them.". And you can see their point. But life isn't like that.

You need to build testing into your estimate and explain that the client and their team will need to test all functionality at some point in the process. Bear in mind that the better something works when they see it, the happier the client.

It is best to test on at least a Mac and a PC and in a few different browsers. My minimum would be Explorer, Safari, Chrome and Firefox.

There are some great websites, some paid, which help show what your website looks like on different platforms and browsers. Use them. Don't underestimate the importance of compatibility.

During the testing stage, development should stop. This is a milestone and the people tasked with performing the testing should have the tools and systems to document what they find.

Bug track

You, your team and the client need to record all the bugs, the broken functionality or inconsistent rendering of the pages. There are some fab online tools for this, or you can just shove it in a spreadsheet. Record the page URL (you can copy that from the browser bar), note the error and give it a priority. A small misalignment of an item on the page will not be as vital as the search function not working, for instance.

Browser: essentially there are three major players in the browser wars. But don't underestimate how many more are out there.

You can do this in a spreadsheet, in a Google Doc (which you can share with the client) or there are stacks of online tools that do lots more. With bugs that are hard to describe or are visual errors, do a screen snapshot or print screen ('prt scn' on a PC or Command Shift 3 on a Mac) and attach it to the bug listing, then the developer can see what you are harping on about.

It is important to capture everybody's comments in one place and in one version, otherwise it gets mighty complicated. Make this very clear to all involved in the project, set a date for the testing to be completed, and correlate all the comments and bugs into one file. This is a milestone, so do whatever you can to make it as complete and as thorough as it can be. Nobody will ever catch everything first time around – them's the breaks, but the more you can do to gather up a good, comprehensive set of comments and revisions, the faster and better the result will be.

It is likely that you will have to go through a few rounds of testing. Make sure each round has a version number and has significant points in a project lifecycle, called milestones. These should be detailed in your schedule, and testing rounds are 'milestones'.

Once all the fixes have been done, you can go through the bug list and check that they have all been done. Occasionally, one bit of functionality will interfere with another bit of functionality and when that bit of functionality gets fiddled with, occasionally, a piece of code over the other side of the site will 'break'. They don't do it on purpose, but it does happen. So whilst one thing might work one day, another thing might not. So during every milestone, the site needs to be checked and double-checked to make sure everything is still working, even if it was working before. An example of this might be if a headline on a sign up form changes on the home page and, let's say it adds a word or two, then on the home page, that might render OK. But that same little piece of functionality could be buried deep within the site and perhaps the column width is a bit narrower and that headline now falls over the form fields. See what I mean? I'll show you.

Don't confuse bugs with changes in the spec; clients like to slip in a change request under the guise of a bug. A bug is something that does not work as it is supposed to, a change request is a change in the requirements.

This register panel is from the same design on page 59. You will note that I have put the form field names in the fields themselves, which causes extra dev work, but for a small form that's OK.

Change requests

The title should give the game away. This is when over the course of a project the client realises that, in actual fact, they want something to be done in a different way, other than what they asked for and you have agreed. Sometimes, it's just because the scoping hasn't been thought out thoroughly enough. Other times it's just because now they can see the thing working, they want it to work another way and they realise something needs to change.

On small projects with tight budgets, try to accommodate what you can, but inevitably, changes to the spec will mean more cost. This must be communicated to the client there and then. Turning up with a bill that is 20 per cent more than you quoted at the end of the project causes big problems and your client is likely to dispute the charges if you are not clear from the outset. I harped on about this on page 170.

Deploy

Under normal circumstances, the site will be built and uploaded to a test sever, and the development work gets uploaded to that server. When all is tip-top and Bristol fashion, the client will sign off and the code can go live and it then gets deployed to the live server. To split hairs, the term 'deploy' means any upload of the code, not just at the end of the project but during the project.

I'm afraid you can't just slope off to the pub now and celebrate – you can soon – but not just yet. Despite the fact that the live website is an exact copy of the test server website, things can still break, so it still needs to be checked.

User or acceptance testing

Clients who spend a lot of money on sites want to make sure that their customer base can actually use the thing. Best way to do that is to get a few users in front of it and let them have a play with it and see what happens. There are companies that specialise in this work, like PEN testing, and there are companies and just test websites. There are a lot of different ways of doing this, as a designer all that you will be concerned about is the results. If the results come back that 90 per cent of users failed to understand the navigation, you are in big trouble. But that is unlikely if you have actually read this book and implemented the principles. User testing is an important step, it can throw up some very interesting things and, like market testing products, it can shape the way the site works and looks. I will leave it at that I think.

Testing is usually performed by asking the panel of testers to perform tasks through a user journey. For instance, you may ask them to "Buy a silk tie and braces." and off they go. The whole thing is often recorded so that the analysts can watch what people do and marvel at how stupid most users are.

Soft launch

A soft launch sounds like you might do this from a bouncy castle, which would be a lot more fun. I think all websites should be launched from a bouncy castle but, to date, browsers do not support this platform.

A soft launch usually means that the site has been put live, but nobody is telling anyone just yet. The links gets shared with a select few. These privileged people have a play with it and occasionally something crops up that isn't right, and perhaps the odd fix or change request takes place. It is a stage that ensures that everybody who cares has seen the site, used it, and is happy for the rest of the world to join in.

Launch

OK, now you can crack open the champagne. The site goes live, the whole world can see it – job done.

PEN testing

This section is about understanding the process of a successful web design and build project. You will have guessed by now that it all depends on the size of the project, how deep your client's pockets are, how much things matter to them, whether a particular activity takes place or not. Your local hairdresser is unlikely to require PEN testing, but your new website for the CIA probably will.

Other pen testing: *is usually done by making a scribble in the corner.*

PEN testing or, to give its full sexual sounding title, penetration testing, basically checks the security of a website and sees if it can be compromised in some way. This whole section reads like some kind of sex scandal and I suppose when big important sites get hacked and people's details get stolen, then it is a bit of a scandal.

Specialist companies perform PEN testing, they have teams of shady people who know way too much about the internet – who poke away at websites and see if they can wheedle their way in via back doors and glitches in the Matrix.

The report comes back and the dev team do things, I have no idea what – they close loop holes, add patches and perhaps some embroidery. Who knows? But when all is said and done, after a PEN test, your site is safe and sound. You and your client can sleep at night and all is good with the world.

Most of the time, sites with sensitive data will require security patches and software upgrades to keep out baddies who have nothing else to do in their lives but try to disrupt websites and read or download important data like your fishing bait preferences. Go for it, lads. Whilst you are sitting in your bedroom hacking away, I've gone fishing.

Support and maintenance

Websites that use databases and CMS software that needs updating or upgrading over time, require a maintenance package, which is usually charged as a monthly fee. Security patches will come out every now and then and have to be updated to help stop baddies hacking into the site. New versions of software are released onto the market and these patches and upgrades need to be installed and upgraded. So that's why clients pay for maintenance.

Maintenance can also mean updates. If you or your company have been tasked with keeping the website up to date, adding new content, editing old content, then this is usually charged on a monthly basis based on the likely amount of time it will take. Obviously, if a whole new bit of functionality is required, this usually falls out of the monthly update remit and you have to scope and estimate.

Support (or technical support) is not the same thing as maintenance, but they often get presented to the client together. After the site is launched, some users need support. For instance, the client has a team of content editors using the CMS and they may get stuck and need help using the system. Support packages come in all shapes and sizes, from a quick email, to live chat or a 24-hour response support desk. This is not usually a job for us designers, but occasionally we have to step in and explain one thing or another.

What usually goes wrong

I'm quite a positive person, but things do go wrong. And more so with web projects than any other design project. The basic reason, which underlines most issues, is people just assume. You may have gathered this from previous chapters and the fact that I have laboured this point to death. Sorry about that.

One result of making assumptions can be resolved by managing expectations and understanding the real world. It's rare to work with people who manage and understand web projects, and know the reality and the potential pitfalls, to be honest. Most clients are business owners or marketing bods and will apply the same attitude and working practices to a web project as they would any other business practices. But a web project just isn't the same.

So, all I can do is list a few things to be aware of, most of which I've either warned you about before or at least given you the processes to help avoid. It doesn't hurt to repeat things, does it? I say, it doesn't hurt – to repeat things?

The internet is free, isn't it?

Yes, it is. But when you ask a client exactly what they want from a website, they often just select everything they can think of, including a host of things they possibly don't need but, hey, they'll have it anyway. So, you end up with clients selecting forums and live chat for their homemade pie business. These things all cost. So advise them on what they really need and price things individually so that they think about their needs and choose what they want.

It's urgent

Everything is urgent. Clients will push you to meet their deadlines and will pressure you to get the job done, no matter what. They will often resist doing the job properly from their end, and avoid things like scoping because it is time consuming. Sometimes, to get the job, you have to agree to a schedule, but you should know and let them know from the start that meeting these deadlines will depend on them doing their job and things going smoothly. This is a really tricky balancing act. Early doors during the project discussions try to agree as much as you can. If you do not accept their initial schedule, they will go elsewhere, because 99 times out of a 100 the client will be under pressure to deliver. 99 times out of a 100, that initial schedule will change as the project proceeds. So caveat to death... you will meet the schedule as long as they meet their side of the bargain.

I've changed my mind

Sure you have, and that is fine, but whilst your client will accept that extra work from their lawyer costs more, for some reason extra work from the designer and developer shouldn't cost any more. Hmm...

You missed the deadline

Usually part of the 'it's urgent' problem. Keep a track of your schedule and any slips. If missing a deadline is you or your team's fault, you should have allowed enough time in your schedule to catch up. If the client has slipped, note it and gently explain.

You never told me
I have my development team sitting probably five metres away from me and emailing me queries. My client is in another office, sometimes in another country. Don't rely on email, pick up the phone, meet face to face, do whatever it takes to keep communication channels open and regular. Remember, your client will be sitting in her office and without keeping her up to date, she may assume that nothing is happening.

Why doesn't it work?
The best level of service delivery is to deliver on time with a fully functioning product. Focus on that, as it's hard to deliver even that most of the time. So make sure you are on the ball and ensure that this idea is in the forefront of your mind. When planning your schedule, allow time for stages of redevelopment and additional testing. Do your upmost to ensure the functionality is working to the highest degree. You won't get thanked for a good job, but you will get shouted at for a bad one.

I've designed what I want in PowerPoint
Oh dear. This client doesn't want to employ a web professional, they want to employ somebody who has the technical skills that they don't have, to build what they have in mind. Politely say 'no, thank you'. Life's too short and you'll never make them happy and you can be absolutely sure you will be miserable.

Ways of working

There was a time when it was dead straightforward, the client told you what they wanted and you gave them a price. Then they changed their minds and decided they didn't want that after all. They have less budget than before, but would like the 'moon on a stick'. So, you'd agree a timeframe which absolutely needed to be met, unless the client went on holiday. Now there are a number of ways of working, each agency has their own rules and each project requires its own particular attention.

Fixed price
Most projects are performed under a fixed price system. This means that you and your client come to an agreement. They stipulate what they want and you tell them how much it costs. That's it. Most of the time, that's fine. I've mentioned change requests, a good idea is to suggest a contingency fund in the budget. You may not get one, but at least you have highlighted that things change and it's best to prepare for them in the early stages. Try to highlight any variables that may incur an additional cost.

Time and materials
This is when a client chooses to pay a web designer, or more often a developer, in chunks of time. The materials bit is a bit hard to identify as code is code and rarely are designers and developers asked to use timber, plaster and paint to build a website. Essentially, it means that the client pays for the time the team spend doing the work and they pay until it is done.

It is important when working under this system to feedback to the client regularly what time has been spent on what activity. A good way of doing this is to use a time tracking tool that details the activities and the hours spent. Generally, the more open you are, the more understanding clients are about the costs.

Sprints: agile phases are broken down into sprints or iterations.

Agile
What a great name, agile. Ready to pounce – fit, lithe and alert. An agile project is a project where the whole team works together in an interactive way. Essentially, this means things change over time and the team adapts to those changes. There is a whole theory behind this (look it up) and a process behind it. Agile is used in software development and tends to be used on large-scale, long-term projects.

Scrum
The term scrum is used in conjunction with an Agile framework. It tackles issues in an iterative, step-by-step process during the development process.

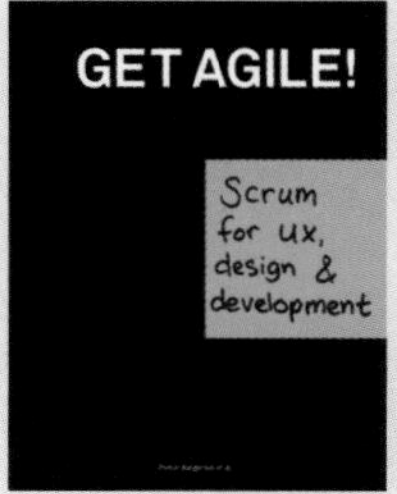

An excellent book produced by a fine publisher.

KNOWLEDGE OF THE WEB

In this day and age, the internet is such an integral part of our lives it is hard to imagine life without it. It used to be that if you wanted to find out who Tim Berners-Lee is, you'd have to traipse off to the library. Now, of course, you can just search his name and the internet will tell you in a flash and for free.

So, I'm guessing you know how the internet works. This chapter aims to help explain how the bits fit together and how these bits relate to web design and build. I'll explain what the bits are first and then we will put them together in a few scenarios that apply to your working life.

Host/server

A host is a machine connected to a network, in our case the World Wide Web. Your website's files, the images, HTML, CSS, etc., have to 'live' somewhere so that when users want to view your pages, they connect to the server these files are sitting on and can download them into the browser for viewing.

Hosting packages come in a huge range of sizes, types and related costs. You can host your website for free, or it can cost thousands a month. Big companies have their own servers, but most websites buy hosting services in.

The charges are often based on the size of the server needed, how much memory it has, and sometimes the amount of traffic or data transfer your site will use.

Often when you buy a domain name, you are offered cheap hosting to go along with it. You don't have to take it.

Mail server

As the name suggests, this server manages your email. Again, mail services often get bundled in with other hosting services or when you buy a domain name.

IP address

An IP address is a number assigned to a machine that is connected to the internet. They are odd little numbers that look like this: 88.208.252.193.

Domain name

A domain name is the web address and often part of the email address that your company has chosen for itself. The domain name 'points' to the IP address, so that when your users type in www.knowyouronions.info they arrive at your website, sitting on the server.

The thing to remember here is a domain name is little more than a forwarding address. If I was stupid enough to change my domain every week, I could have for instance, www.anotherdomain.com pointing to my website and the next week change it to www.ihavechangedmydomain.com. A domain name is just a label or sticker, nothing more.

Of course, everybody wants a great domain name; if you sell jeans, then www.jeans.com is brilliant. But other people had the same idea (back in 1992) and it is likely that a domain like that has been registered. When you are working for a client, you may get asked to advise on the domain choice. You will have to search to see if the domains and names you want have been taken. This can often end up in what can only be described as 'domain name shoehorning', where the only domain left is something along the lines of www.we-sell-jeans.net; this happened with Know Your Onions. All the domains that I wanted had gone so I had to resort to .info. Not ideal, but then that's life.

There are a number of things you can do to get around domains that have gone. You can choose an odd affix, more on this later. You can add in another word. Films do this all the time, www.batman-themovie.com. You can add a hyphen, or you can think out of the box. Thinking out of the box eventually creates its own box, of course, and that is why we have websites called gazoink.com, poopla.com and other meaningless names.

When I started my company, Navig8 was taken, so for the first few years until I was able to snaffle it, I went with navig8the.net. But the best names are the simple ones and must include the company's name. This brings me to the domain name extensions.

Domain name extensions

There are so many that I'm not going to attempt to list them. I'll explain the basics. Domains are broken into two types, Top Level Domains (TLD), these are country domains, or, well, look it up – the other category I will call 'other'. Some rules apply where you are restricted by the country you are in, but mostly common sense should be applied.

Domain list: Wikipedia has a very comprehensive list if you need it.

For instance, .net is really a network domain, but I used it because it worked for me. The Know Your Onions website uses .info domain, as I figured this was a better option than www.knowyouronions-webdesign.com, for instance.

I will tackle a few definitions of what the extensions are meant to be for, but in good old internet fashion, the rules are flounced.

.com company, tends to be seen as the global domain and great if you bag that along with all the others.

.org is for organisations and can be followed by a country extension like.org.uk

.ac is for education organisations and again can be followed by a country extension.

.mobi gets used for mobile sites.

.xxx is relatively new (the governing body releases new extensions now and then), but I can't remember what it's used for.

You get the idea. It's best when searching to check that the domain you want has the extensions you need available and it is best to buy them all. If other people have some of the domains, it's a good idea to check that, if your customers stumble on the wrong site by accident, it's not going to be a major embarrassment.

Lastly, take a long hard look at how the domain looks written out; I mention this in *Know Your Onions: Graphic Design*. There have been some fantastic oversights, for example:

www.kidsexchange.net which was meant to read kids exchange, but may not to some readers.

www.therapistfinder.com is a directory of therapists, maybe.

www.speedofart.com I wish this was a swimwear site, but no, it's the speed of art.

There's plenty more and you wouldn't want to be in a situation working for Pen Island and registered an address that could be read in perhaps a way you hadn't intended.

Whois

Whois is a way of searching in the records to see who owns a domain. If you are an individual, you can opt out so your details aren't listed.

ISP

ISP stands for Internet Service Provider, these companies are the ones you pay to let you access the internet. They provide the link between your computer and the big old World Wide Web, and leave you on hold when you call them.

FTP

File Transfer Protocol, sounds like a very good 1960s spy film. "Jeremy, code named the Stallion, obtained the files from his contact in Istanbul, getting them to our man in Havana using the File Transfer Protocol." Sadly not, this is the usual way that developers upload the files to the server. You can do it too, it's a bit like emailing or just copying a file, all you need is a thing called an FTP client. I don't know why they are called clients, but they are. There are lots of free ones out there. FTP is the standard way to upload files onto your server.

Database

If you think of a database like a big spreadsheet, you are not far off. As the name suggests, it is where the data lives, but it can also hold code and other bits and bobs. Databases are hosted independently from the main site and can be accessed using a control panel, called a C-Panel to make it sound a little more *Star Trek*.

Control panel

Unless you start tinkering with development and code, you may not have a need to access the control panel, or C-Panel. This is an interface that allows the developers to manage and configure the hosting of the website.

Cloud computing

Cloud computing or hosting means something and nothing really. Loosely, it means a network of computers, with data stored remotely, as opposed to locally, on your own computer. To access your files (which can be anything from music to your website) you need an internet connection. This often means running around like a maniac trying to find a WiFi spot when you are on holiday.

Connection addiction: at this point you might realise how much you use the internet.

Because our data is sitting up there in the sky, we can access our files on all our different devices, iPads, phones and computers.

Applications and programmes can run 'in the cloud' and I suspect one day the world will be covered by one big internet and we will be seamlessly connected to it 24 hours a day and not even realise it.

I know this is all basic stuff and some of you will be rolling your eyes and muttering, but some people, even though they use this technology, don't know how it works. Onwards.

KNOWLEDGE OF THE TEAM

There are often a lot of people involved in a big web project, or it could just be you, the client and the developer. It is handy to know what the different technologies and programming languages do, as well as what some of the various roles and job titles mean.

Project Manager

PMs are the people that steer the ship through the choppy waters. PMs liaise with the client, the design team and the developers, to make sure everybody knows what is going on and tries and keep the project on schedule.

A lot of agencies cover these fees in their estimate or charge a percentage of the final cost. A good, highly organised PM is a valuable asset as they deal with all the things that you probably don't want to deal with. A bad PM will sink a ship. Small projects mean all the project management work is down to you. I tell you how to do this in the section called 'Working'.

Developers

Developers are programmers, but they like to be called developers. They come in all shapes and sizes, as does everybody. It is rare to find a developer who can do everything. They tend to choose a language or skill, either PHP or ASP, front end, back end or whatever.

The bigger the development team, the more specialised the developer's skills tend to be. It's not unusual for a developer to just be responsible for theming or front end development, for instance. Smaller teams need developers who do the lot.

Content editors

These are the people who write and edit the content for the website. They usually come in various levels of importance. So a lowly content editor might write articles that need to be queued in the system for their boss to come along and check all is tickety-boo before it goes live.

UX designer

A User Experience designer tends to work on interfaces for applications, websites or any Graphic User Interface (GUI) and understands the whole human interaction and all the issues that go with that. They deal with the wireframing, the information architecture, everything that affects the user experience. They is experts, innit. UI is the same thing, it just means User Interface.

You, as a web designer, will deal with some of these issues yourself or perhaps work with a UX designer. Obviously, if you assume the title, then you have chosen your specialism, but you will need to learn all that is involved before you can really call yourself an expert. So don't go claiming you are a UX expert unless you is, innit.

System analyst

These are technical bods who understand how to join up all the different data and functional parts of a website. They are very technical and talking to them, or at least listening to them, can make you feel you have landed in a parallel universe, where the inhabitants only use some of the words you know, but with different meanings, like stack, proxy, ping, compile and dilithium.

Webmaster

When you say webmaster, you have to say it in a voice of a dark villain, 'I am the webmaster, you must obey'. It's actually a bit of an odd title, really. I think it was originally meant for a more technical role, so you might need to change your voice in those circumstances, but generally, these people are tasked with being responsible for the site or sites. They are the boss.

Search Engine Optimisation expert types

These types sort of float about really, they feed into the content editors work, so that they use the right search terms in their content. They also structure page titles and URLs with the development team and liaise with the client to ensure the content fits with what they want to say, as well as performing well for the search engines. Each term is assessed to deliver the highest level of search against the lowest competition. All this hocus pocus helps make sure the right customers are looking at their site.

Keyword (?) (40)	Searches (?) (N/A)	Competition (?)	IAAT (?)	KEI (?)
jigsaw (search)	110,000	48	45,000	67.6
jigsaw puzzles (search)	40,500	37	4,040	66.7
the jigsaw puzzles (search)	2,900	8	6	65.2
jigsaw puzzle (search)	2,900	43	13,400	39.4
jigsaw games (search)	2,400	22	130	38.9
jigsaw puzzle games (search)	1,600	26	363	50.0
personalised jigsaw (search)	880	11	12	38.9
photo jigsaw (search)	880	0	0	0
jigsaw puzzles games (search)	880	15	29	55.9
jigsaw puzzles uk (search)	720	0	0	0
jigsaw puzzles for kids (search)	590	0	0	0
jigsaw puzzles for adults (search)	590	0	0	0
national geographic jigsaw (search)	590	0	0	0
kids jigsaw puzzles (search)	390	13	17	35.0
wooden jigsaw puzzles (search)	390	19	72	29.6
1000 piece jigsaw puzzles (search)	320	12	14	50.0
national geographic jigsaw puzzles (search)	320	0	0	0
jigsaw london (search)	320	0	0	0
christmas jigsaw puzzles (search)	320	0	0	0
childrens jigsaws (search)	260	0	0	0
personalised jigsaws (search)	260	0	0	0
personalised jigsaw puzzles (search)	210	0	0	0

Searching: *this shows the number of monthly searches and the number of websites competing for these terms.*

SEO is a specialism in itself. Many companies claim to be SEO experts, few are. They say things like, "we do SEO". Really? True SEO requires ongoing effort, a clear strategy and constant change. The world these people live in changes all the time. Search engines are forever refining their algorithms to help people like you and me get what they are looking for when they search for something. SEO experts spend a lot of time keeping on top of things as they change.

I was going to include in this book a chapter about SEO, but then I thought, nah, I know a bit, but a little knowledge is a dangerous thing.

All websites should at least have the basics in place, so that when a search result comes up, at least the company website gets served. If your client wants to be number one, then best to do the job properly.

The client

The person that pays the bills, signs off the work and makes uninformed decisions. ;-) If it wasn't for the client there would be nothing, no day, no night, no rain or light. Whilst your design should focus on your client's client, your working practices, service level and relationships should all be focused on them.

On the seventh day he rested: I'm sounding quite biblical here.

10 THINGS...

...a client will do to mess up 'your' site post launch

1. They will write content that will be way too long, even if you tell them not to.
2. They will upload clip art to 'illustrate' an article which will be wholly inappropriate.
3. They will say 'I didn't realise' and blame you for not realising when a change in spec means more work.
4. They will blame you for not thinking of everything for them, so think of it as your job.
5. Make 'small changes to the spec' that have huge functionality issues and get very upset when you suggest they might have to pay extra.
6. They will tell you that the site is absolutely, very urgent and must be live by a certain date and then miss all their deadlines to deliver.
7. No matter how well the job goes, they will say that the project hasn't gone as they had expected. Unless you get every single step and stage 100 per cent right.
8. They will not understand the value, purpose or cost of ongoing maintenance.
9. At every stage, no matter what you tell them, they will focus on the minutia; if you have spelt their name wrong, nothing on the page will matter more than that.
10. If you make them look good to their bosses, they will love you forever. This is your ultimate goal.

10 THINGS...

...a web designer wishes a developer would do

1. Check their work.
2. Test their work.
3. Erm, test and check their work.
4. Tell you what is the longest deadline, not what they hope to achieve.
5. Engage in the team and communicate early on what they need.
6. Flag up problems early and offer a work around or an alternative solution.
7. Remember that some people use Macs.
8. Grasp the nettle and advise a client rather than push back and ask what the client wants, they don't always know what they want, bless 'em.
9. Sometimes a simple solution will do, try to explain the solution.
10. Remember we don't know how it works, so take the time to explain in a way we might begin to understand. Explain it like you are talking to your Grandma.

10 THINGS...

...a developer wishes a web designer would do

1 Make it easier for images to export from Photoshop, especially ones with shadows as they cause difficulties.

2 When designing, don't forget error pages, like validation errors for forms and login errors, etc. – these need to be designed too.

3 Make text in PSDs selectable (not rasterised) which makes it difficult to know font sizes and weight, etc.

4 When using proprietary fonts (not web safe) you need to be supplied with the font file itself. Note that some of these fonts may require permission or licence to be used in a website, please do the research before using them.

In this context semantic means to a standard.

5 Styling a select list is difficult; they need to be converted to an unordered list and then style them. This is not semantic, because they cannot be selected by pressing the tab key.

6 Allow enough time for development, sometimes it cannot be done quicker.

7 Correlate all of your comments into a spread sheet or something similar.

8 Remember to allow us time to learn new things.

9 Tell us at the beginning what browser support you require.

10 Remember, a responsive website takes longer to build and much longer to test.

By Vishu Srinivasan

10 THINGS...

...a client wishes a web designer would do

1. Learn what matters to each client. Don't assume that the price or costs are their main driver. It is for some, but other clients need quality or something else.

2. Remember that your vision as a designer might not allow for all of the factors that concern your client. They may choose the 'wrong' design, but that might still be right.

3. Listen.

4. Do get to know your client so you can tell when they are really panicked or when something really, really matters to them.

5. Don't think that being charming or buying gifts keeps clients. Good work brings clients back and a returning client is worth twice as much as a new one.

6. When pitching, do what you were asked to do in the brief. There is a time to be clever. It's after you did what you were asked to do, not before.

7. Do tell your client the truth, particularly when you think they are mistaken or don't need what they asked for. Clients value that. Just do it when there is no one in the room that will criticise them (like their boss!).

8. Most clients are not as sophisticated as you are in their aesthetic appreciation of the finer points of design. In that sense, they are more like normal people than you are.

9. Remember, what you do and what they do is a job. The client seldom wants the same things to be perfect that you do.

10. If they come back, you did a good job.

By Timothy Barnes, gift client to all small businesses and Director, Enterprise Operations, University College London

10 THINGS...

...a project manager wishes a web designer would do

1. Actually look at the schedule and comment early if things might be difficult to achieve.
2. Keep the schedule in mind during the project and check it regularly.
3. Stick to the schedule!
4. Advise very early on if there is going to be a delay.
5. Keep the PM informed, if a conversation outside of their ears takes place (come to think of it, if they happened within their ears, it would be very odd), make sure the decisions and discussions get fed back.
6. Take responsibility for your own role.
7. Be ready and accept change.
8. Remember we are on the same side.
9. We may not be aware of the implications of some design changes, so educate us, if you want us to understand.
10. Don't blame the PM!

10 THINGS...

...an art director wishes a web designer would do

1. Take a good hard look at the brand and design for the market.
2. Work up rough designs, use a pencil and a pad first, then show us style examples.
3. Don't steal from the internet.
4. Back up your work.
5. Name your files properly.
6. Commit to an elements page, understand them and do them.
7. Be accurate; 1 pixel out and it will show.
8. Understand the nature of the process; help all the team to pull together.
9. Be inquisitive – and never assume.
10. Take responsibility for the project.

10 THINGS...

...an account director wishes a web designer would do

Non-disclosure agreement, i.e. keep your mouth shut.

1. Aspire to be a great designer, seems everyone wants to be a director, rather than a doer these days.

2. Exercise an NDA at the pub. And if there is no NDA, remember, clients drink in pubs too.

3. Avoid plugging into your headphones, it disconnects you from the team and team banter is where the magic happens.

4. Understand your PM is your own personal conduit to looking cool.

5. Strategy is fundamental. But it's more important you recognise the tasks that don't need strategic thinking than those that do.

6. Design is an end-to-end process across the whole business; share your thinking as much as you can, wherever you can.

7. Never be a media banner snob, the best designers are those who make all things mundane be beautiful.

8. Behave like the client's customer. Go into their stores, shop their products, plug in to their social conversations etc, etc.

9. There's no other way to say this. Accept that sometimes purely commercial decisions are the motive for a design change. Boo hoo.

10. And if you really want to stand out, don't buy a Soho label tee, wear Diesel jeans, or have a Japanese girlfriend.

By Lisa* Mesztig

Lisa always signs with an asterix, I don't know why.

10 THINGS...

...a boss wishes a web designer would do

1. Voice an opinion, but try not to argue.
2. Design appropriately, but that doesn't mean without creativity.
3. Never copy, it's OK to have influences though.
4. Follow the process because when you say, "I thought it would be quicker if I just..." it won't be.
5. Understand we have a business to run and occasionally that means making money.
6. If there is an issue, about anything, come and see us as soon as you can – it's our job to fix issues.
7. You can't always choose who you work with and you can't choose the clients, but treat them professionally, that usually gets around most situations.
8. Working from home is nice and you get to stay in your pyjamas, but it's better when you are in the studio, working as part of the team.
9. Be loyal, we took a leap of faith employing you, prove us right.
10. Have fun.

COLLOQUIALISMS

My writing style is kinda chatty and I use sayings a lot. This books gets sold all over the world and some people might not know what I mean by Clobber. This will help them.

Anchor man: is a term that means a figurehead, somebody who knows what they are doing.

Bang on about: keep repeatedly mentioning until it is really boring.

Benefits in spades: a huge amount of benefits.

Bonkers: crazy.

Bouncing when they visited the website: when a user arrives at a website they leave.

Bugs: errors in the code or functionality and display that does not work.

Chill: kick back, chill, take it easy.

Change request: anything that is outside the agreed spec where a deliverable changes.

Clobber: clothes.

Content is King: the ideal that content within a website is the most important thing to make it successful.

Content type: the various types of content.

Contingency fund: an amount of money set aside in the budget to allow for variables in the project delivery – after all, things do change.

Covers your arse: doing or saying something so that you will not be held responsible.

Crack on: get on with the task in hand.

Dodgy: not to be trusted.

Downsampled: in our world this means to reduce the quality of the output.

Drill down: look at the finer points of an issue.

Easy peasy: very easy to do.

Fat footers: sections on a website, at the bottom of a page that tend to hold large amounts of links.

Flashsterbation: the over use of Flash animations for no apparent reason other than showing off.

Fresh eyes: somebody who will look at something and has the benefit of not having seen it before. This gives them an untainted view.

Gawd: my God, my gosh.

Get their head round: begin to understand.

Grasp the nettle: deal with the problem.

Hand gesture: an interaction with a hand or finger movement, usually associated with a tablet or smart phone.

Harped: keep going on about.

Kaput: broken.

Kicks the bucket: dead.

Lightbox: in the web world this is a panel that loads over the top of a web page to show an image or a gallery of images.

Light your fire: make you happy.

Locally: this means developing or working on your own computer's hard drive and not online.

Milestones: points in a project that are defining, things like sign off on the design work, functionality and best of all – the invoice.

Nitty gritty: the real detail

No great shakes for them: it does not really matter to them, they don't care.

Nose out of joint: if they have their nose out of joint, then they are unhappy.

Off the mark: you have missed the point.

Opening a tin of worms: an issue that once you address it creates a whole host of other issues that need to be dealt with.

Pan out: the way things might turn out to be.

PEN testing: to test a website to see if you can compromise its security.

Pixel perfect: to design and build to a point that is 100 per cent perfect in terms of measurement – in our case the pixel.

Powers that be: the people who decide what you do.

Proprietary systems: anything that requires you to use a system that is controlled by somebody else.

Responsive: the way that content can be presented to a user, no matter what device or platform they might have and enable them to have the best possible user experience.

Rupert: this is my invention, I mean bottom. I am so sorry for every Rupert out there.

Literally: or as they say in America, a can of worms.

This section is for my overseas readers. It may be obvious to you what 'chill' means, but perhaps not to a reader in Hong Kong.

Silk purse out of a sow's ear: make something good out of something not so good.

Slices: in our world this is a section taken from a Photoshop document, cut out and saved as a graphic.

Snaffle: to take in a sneaky way.

Soft launch: this is when you put your brand spanking new website live, but you don't promote it and only tell a select few. A lot of people use this stage as a last minor test and tidy up.

Split hairs: argue or deliberate over tiny matters.

That is the rub: that is the issue.

Tickety-boo: going well and in good order.

Tip-top and Bristol fashion: in excellent shape and in full working order.

Tomfoolery: messing around.

Under the hood: the inner workings.

Uppity: annoyingly arrogant.

Up town top ranking: really good, the best.

Ways to skin a cat: as in there are a number ways to skin a cat, meaning there are lots of ways to do the same thing.

Willy nilly: all over the place, doing some thing without order.

Yonks: a long time.

GLOSSARY

Yesh, a glossary of internet terms, where do you start? I will make a start but there is no way I'll be able to finish, but hey, that is what the internet is good for, looking things up. I will jot down some useful ones because I can at least explain them in terms of a designer and of course make lame jokes.

A is for Apple
An Apple is a well-designed, easily transportable, minimalist piece of fruit. The entire object is beautifully designed for its sole purpose, as opposed to pineapples, which sound like they are from the same family, but are difficult to use and have lots of additional accessories (unnecessary). Efforts to make pineapples easier to use mean they have to be manipulated into pineapple chunks (PCs) which is a poor solution and break down or turn to mush over time. At the centre of every Apple is its core, which houses some chips, sorry pips, which, in time, go on to produce the next generation of Apples.

Back save
This is when you have to save a file format in an earlier version so that people who do not have the most up-to-date software version can open the file.

Bleed
This is a print term really, meaning the image or colour goes to the edge of the printed page. It is used to describe a background in a browser that always fills the window, no matter the size of the window.

Resolution
Determines the amount of information in a given area. Measured in pixels per inch. 72ppi is the standard web resolution.

Pixels
The smallest amount of graphic information used to make up an image.

RGB
Stands for Red, Green and Blue. The three colours a monitor uses to make full colour images.

Monitor
Basically, a screen.

Fixed width
A design that has a predetermined width.

Fluid
A design that changes its dimensions to suit the user's device or window size.

Float
A term used when positioning something. An item or web page can float in the window. CSS coders use floats to position items in code, instead of positioning them absolutely.

PSD
Photoshop document.

User testing
A process where your web designs are tested by users to see if they are able to use it intuitively and if they use the functions as intended.

Acceptance testing
This is when a piece of software, code or a website is tested to see if it meets the requirements.

Live text
Text on a website that is editable and not made of graphics.

Rollover states
How an item reacts when a mouse hovers over the item, usually a link. Sometimes called a 'hover state'.

Hover state
See rollover state.

Microsite
A small site, away from the main site, that performs a particular function. They are often branded differently.

CMS
Content Management System, a piece of software that allows the users to update content without any, or little, knowledge of code.

Open source
Software that is offered for free distribution by very nice people (a lot of them have goatee beards).

Linux
An open source operating system. Android is another.

Android
An open source software platform from Google.

MySql
An open source database.

SQL
A programming language for managing data.

ASP and ASP.NET
Active server pages, a language developed by Microsoft for developing dynamic websites.

Dynamic
A term used when developers are building websites that perform functions or deliver content as they go along, rather than a static site, which is like a couch potato.

On the fly
In our world this means something that changes or does something as you are using it. If a form changes from zip code to postcode because you have entered 'UK', for instance.

Static
A website that does not change its content without someone actively changing it. As opposed to dynamic.

Permissions
For us, this usually relates to what level some user has to change or access a certain page in a CMS or access to a server or system.

H1, H2, etc.
These basically stand for Headline one and so on. Browsers look for some standard styling terms, as do search engines. If you haven't read the section on this in the book, what on earth are you looking in the glossary for?

Contextual links
Links within content, usually live text links. If I had a contextual link in this sentence the underlined word would take you to a web page telling you all about them.

Heavy or Graphic heavy
This means the file sizes on a web page or the download of a page are large, usually because the site has lots of graphics. With Flash, you have to wait for the whole thing to download, which is why you see a loading loop.

Loading loop
Whether it is a circle, an egg timer or a bar, you sit there and wait for the download to finish before you can get on with the business in hand. Video and Flash often use loading loops.

Other meanings: in a hurry or actually on the fly itself, but it would need to be very small.

Front end (development)
Here you are concerning yourself with the design and development of what the end user will see.

Back end (development)
This is all the stuff you can't see, all the code and database that sit in the background making the stuff work.

Tone of voice
This is how the whole thing 'sounds'. Each company has a way of talking about themselves. For example, a kid's online game uses a very different written and visual language to, say, a global bank – just a bit different.

Native file formats
These are the file formats that you work in to originate things. For example a PSD is a native file format, which you might export as a jpeg, which ain't.

Vector
Vector files can be enlarged to any size.

Thanks to:

Navig8 team, Vishu, Patrick, Mr Dinsdale, Joe, Lisa, Tim and all the people who granted permission for me to reproduce their work. In particular UCL and British Council.

Errors or omissions
I welcome any suggestions or corrections you might have.

If I've made a mistake or not credited someone, I unreservedly apologise. Drop me a line and I'll put it right.

Thanks for reading,
Drew
www.knowyouronions.info